QUEER
LONDON

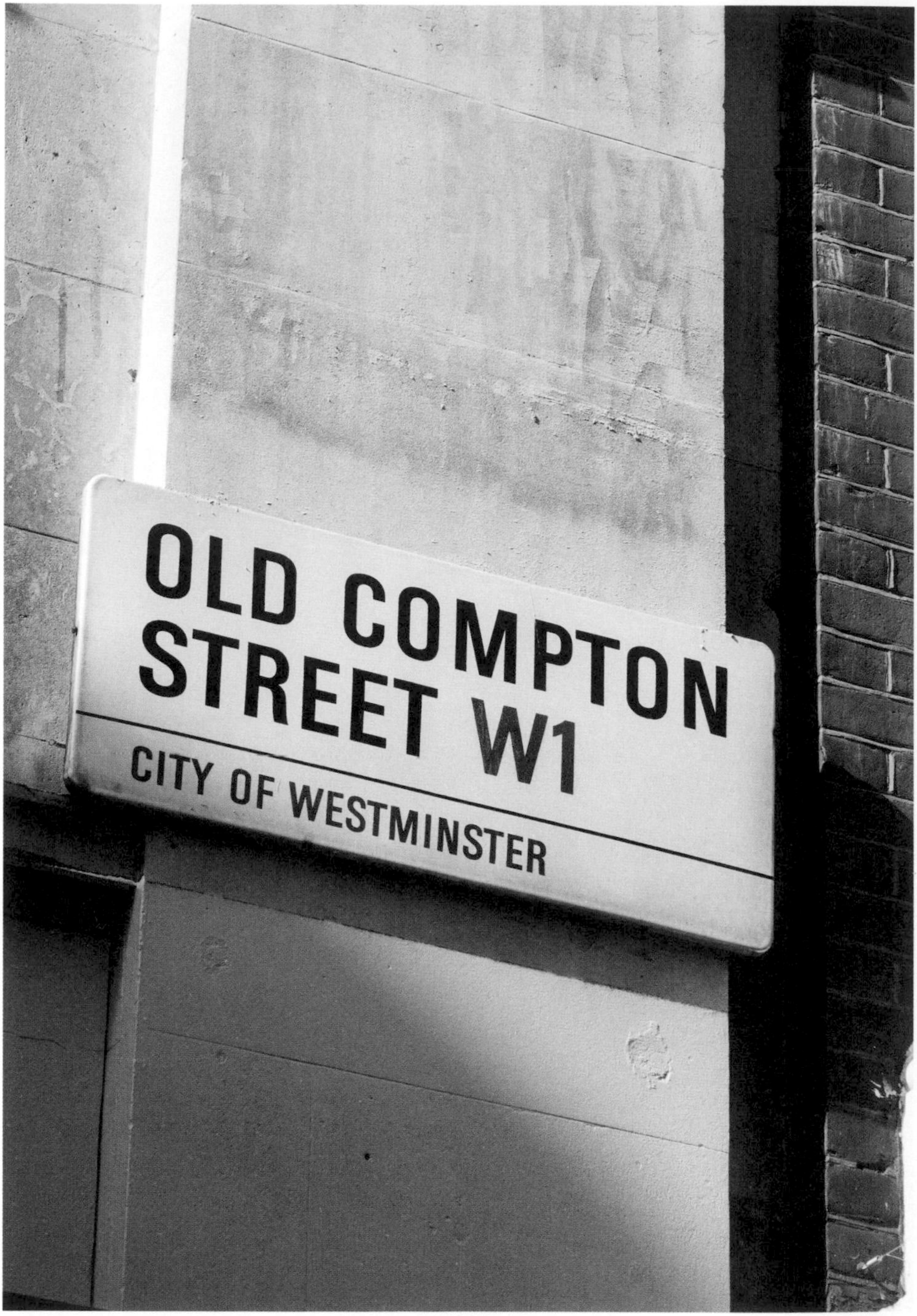
OLD COMPTON
STREET W1
CITY OF WESTMINSTER

QUEER LONDON

A GUIDE TO THE CITY'S LGBTQ+ PAST AND PRESENT

Alim Kheraj

Photographs by Tim Boddy

ACC ART BOOKS

INTRODUCTION

Throughout my life, I've constantly interrogated what exactly 'Queer London' is. Growing up in the '90s under the vice of Section 28 (a Thatcherite law prohibiting the 'promotion of homosexuality'), Soho held an unknowable allure whenever I visited its higgledy-piggledy streets. It maintained that magic as I became a teenager: Soho was where, aged 14, I went alone to my first Pride, only to bump into my Biology teacher on Greek Street. I remember the nervous excitement that hummed through me as I walked with the crowd, soaking up the fact that there were so many LGBTQ+ people in London. The first gay club I went to, Ghetto, was tucked away between the Astoria and Soho Square. Like many queer kids who came of age in the 2000s, my gay education began and ended with *Queer as Folk*. I devoured both the British and American versions, and believed that – like Manchester and the fictional version of Pittsburgh – each city around the world had its own gay village. In my young mind, London's was Soho.

Naturally, that changed. On a night out with my sister, we (rather naively) went to Fire in Vauxhall. It offered a version of what I'd come to know from Soho, but on steroids. Muscular men danced with their tops off, people were clearly on drugs and it was, for me at least, a little much – although none of that stopped me going back. When I returned to London after studying in Brighton, wizened a little to the realities of the gay scene, Soho had lost its shimmer. I started exploring further afield and soon became whisked up by the bars, clubs and alternative queer nightlife of East London. For a time, Shoreditch and Dalston offered me the version of queer life I had read about in Armistead Maupin's *Tales of the City*, albeit one in a different century and with much less sunshine. The anarchic pull of the

Joiners Arms and the creative energy at the George and Dragon were sacred, and I met people there who I am still friends with today. Of course, I still ventured into Soho, finding comfort in spaces like the King's Arms and nostalgia in the basement of Ku Bar and the dance floor of G-A-Y Late. I also started a love affair with the Royal Vauxhall Tavern and Dalston Superstore and The Glory (although, I'll admit that I was not a fan of the Black Cap). These places, many shabby and all with terrible toilets, became a part of me.

However, I also witnessed in real time London's insatiable appetite for change.

Over the years I had spent venturing onto the queer scene, nearly 60% of the city's LGBTQ+ venues closed. This was thanks to a mixture of redevelopment, rising business rates, sky-rocketing rents and changes of ownership. I watched as Ghetto was demolished to make way for Crossrail; saw Madame Jojo's cease to exist in the blink of an eye; and mourned the loss of the Joiners, which – still empty today – was once the epicentre of the East London scene, around which I had started to build my life. My 'Queer London' was being eroded away.

But the disappearance and destruction of these physical spaces woke me up to another aspect of 'Queer London'. While the number of places where LGBTQ+ people congregated were shrinking, a sense of community that I had so far been oblivious to, but which has always existed, came to the fore. Thanks to friends I made on the scene, through my work as a writer and on Twitter, I discovered the incredible work of grassroots LGBTQ+ organisations and queer artistic collectives, as well as an underground, alternative nightlife. This was solidified for me when I wrote an article for *Time Out* magazine about a proposed LGBTQ+ community centre in the city. Here were people from all intersections of the LGBTQ+ community, of every race and age, coming together off their own backs to create space for the city's queer community. In the face of what seemed like 'the beginning of the end' for London's LGBTQ+ scene, they showed me there was hope. My relative privilege as a white-passing mixed-race person and my general disinterest in Pride had made me unaware of UK Black Pride, an essential organisation that both demands and creates space for Black LGBTQ+ people and QTIPOC. 'Queer London' wasn't the bricks and mortar. It was – and is – the people who create and breathe and dance and live, in those spaces and beyond.

Beginning the research for *Queer London,* this was my mentality. I scurried off to the Bishopsgate Institute and pored over old copies of *Gay News, Capital Gay, Kennedy's Gay Guide, London Scene* and all the ephemera I could find. I read history books and, with the help of many, spoke to LGBTQ+ individuals who have been alive since before homosexuality was legal in this country; along with young folx on the frontiers of new queer culture. I learned that corners of London I've barely visited were once hubs of queer life. I read about the lives of people who died during the height of the HIV/AIDS epidemic. I was introduced to the world of Molly houses and proto-drag queens like Princess Seraphina. I eventually came to understand that 'Queer London' was a depthless ocean – one I had dived into head first, swam in for what seemed like miles and yet still only scratched the surface of.

More than anything though, I realised I'd attempted to quantify 'Queer London' in things that were physical. While it is important to incorporate the people and the places and the histories, the defining feature of 'Queer London' is *resilience.* Looking at the lives of LGBTQ+ people and the spaces they've claimed over hundreds of years, I can see how cyclical things are. Not only have queer people been a part of the fabric of the city since its inception, but they have watched the places on which they staked their claim be gobbled up time and time again. And so, they have fought – not only to make room for themselves in a city that's constantly changing, but against persecution and violence, erasure and hate.

I have tried my hardest to capture this in *Queer London.* This book is by no means exhaustive but I hope it proves a useful guide to LGBTQ+ life in the capital. Interspersed with listings of bars, clubs, shops, charities, club nights and community organisations are pockets of history and tales that demonstrate the strength and fortitude of the LGBTQ+ people who have come before me. Writing it hasn't been easy. Aside from the usual difficulties that accompany any project, the global coronavirus pandemic has put up innumerable barriers. As I'm writing this, we don't know what the long-term implications of the virus will be. The pandemic has already affected the city's LGBTQ+ community, be it through the loss of work or illness. I've only been able to maintain some semblance of normality because of the lesson this book taught me: that 'Queer London' has battled fiercer foes. It has been, and will always be, resilient.

Alim Kheraj, London

GLOSSARY OF TERMS

Allosexual

Someone who is not asexual, who experiences sexual attraction.

Ally

A heterosexual, allosexual cisgender individual who supports LGBTQ+ rights, advocates for LGBTQ+ equality and challenges homophobia, biphobia and transphobia.

Bear

A burly and hairy gay or bisexual man of a certain age who presents themselves in a rugged or masculine way. A younger-looking, less rugged version of a bear is known as a cub.

Butch

A person, usually a lesbian, a queer womxn or a non-binary individual, who presents as more masculine and identifies with traits, behaviours or styles aligned with masculinity.

Chemsex

Sexual activity that occurs while under the influence of drugs, often involving multiple partners at parties or hang outs. Drugs associated with chemsex include methamphetamine, GHB/GBL, mephedrone, cocaine and ketamine.

Cisgender

A person whose gender identity corresponds with the sex they were assigned at birth.

Clones

Coined in the late '70s, this term refers to specific masculine look that gay men adopted, usually involving blue denim jeans, plaid shirts, leather jackets and moustaches, that resulted in people looking identical.

Cruising

A term used commonly by gay and bisexual men to describe searching for a sexual encounter with other men, often in a public place.

Drag

The performance of gender expression. For example, a drag queen is someone who performs a heightened version of femininity, while a drag king is someone who performs a heightened version of masculinity.

Femme

The opposite of butch. A person who presents as more feminine and identifies with traits, behaviours and styles aligned with femininity.

Hanky code

A way that men historically communicated with one another in gay bars or discreet environments. Different coloured handkerchiefs worn in specific back pockets (left or right) pertain to different things. For example, a navy-blue hanky in the left pocket signals a 'top' (the giver) while the same hanky in the right pocket signals a 'bottom' (the receiver).

LGBTQIA

Lesbian, Gay, Bisexual, Transgender, Queer, Intersex, Asexual.

Non-binary

A person whose gender identity cannot be defined by the binaries of male or female. Non-binary people can sometimes identify as both male and female or neither male nor female. Non-binary people sometimes, but not always, use they/them pronouns. Other terms used by non-binary people include genderqueer, genderfluid, agender and third gender.

PEP

Post-exposure prophylaxis. This anti-HIV medication may prevent you developing an HIV infection if you have been exposed to the virus. Treatment must begin within 72 hours of coming into contact with the virus.

PrEP

Pre-exposure prophylaxis. A medication taken by HIV-negative people before and after sex that reduces the risk of getting HIV.

QTIBIPOC

Queer, Trans, Intersex, Black, Indigenous, People of Colour.

QTIBPOC

Queer, Trans, Intersex, Black, People of Colour – a more common acronym, in the UK.

Queer

An umbrella term that pertains to any person who is of a sexual or gender minority (i.e., who is not cisgender, allosexual and heterosexual).

Transgender

A person whose gender identity does not correspond with the sex they were assigned at birth.

Womxn

A modification of the word 'woman' that removes the word 'man' to avoid perceived sexism and to signal the inclusion of trans and non-binary people.

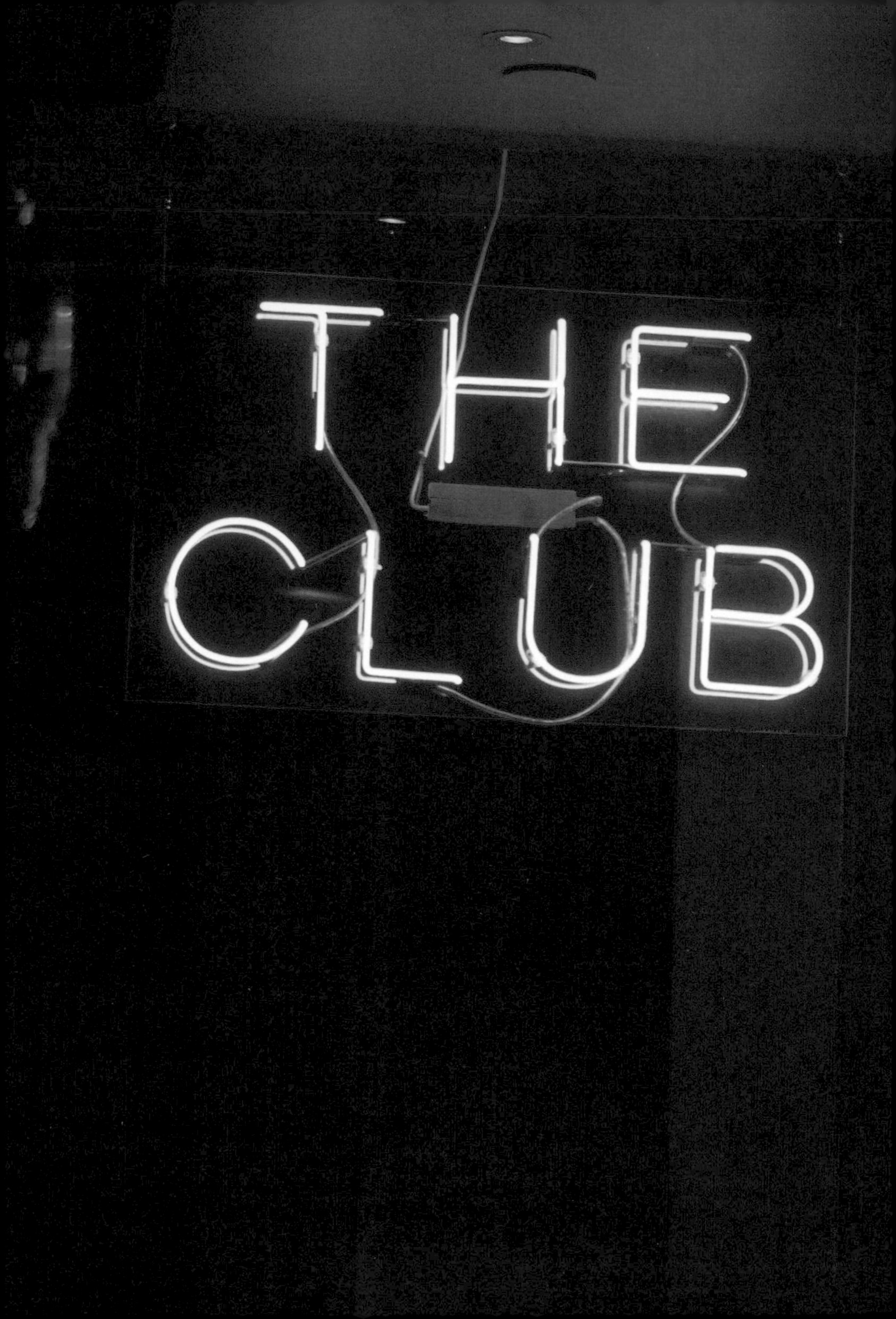
THE
CLUB

NIGHTLIFE

CENTRAL

BARS

THE ADMIRAL DUNCAN
54 Old Compton St, Soho, W1D 4UB
ww.admiral-duncan.co.uk
Nearest Tube: Tottenham Court Road

There has been a pub by this space since the 1800s. During World War II it was hit by a bomb, and up until around the mid-90s it was a fairly standard boozer. It transformed when Soho became London's new gaybourhood – but in 1999, a bomb exploded in the venue, causing widespread injury and three deaths.

However, the Admiral Duncan is more than its history. Thanks to its blue and gold frontage (as well as the ever-present rainbow flag) you can't miss it if you're swishing down Old Compton Street. If you pop in, you'll find a fairly standard pub. There's nothing fancy or pretentious here. A bar runs the length of the rectangular venue. There isn't much in the way of seating, especially at the weekends, when people pack in like gay sardines. At the far end of the room is a stage, and it's here the Admiral Duncan comes into its own.

While other bars and clubs host cabaret and drag performances, the Dunc' has doubled down on its entertainment offerings for well over a decade, becoming one of central London's most reliable spots for quality drag. Queens from *RuPaul's Drag Race UK* make regular appearances, like Baga Chips and Sum Ting Wong. But it's the local favourites – Sandra, so-called 'whore of Hampstead Heath'; and Cosmic – who have helped elevate the Duncan's consistent programme of cabaret and drag. Of course, this is Soho, so you're not going to find the more experimental and subversive drag queens or kings who strut across stages further east. But that's not the audience the Duncan caters to – or what you'd venture into Soho to find, in a district that has comfortably settled into its dameship and relinquished its edginess. Not that there's anything wrong with that.

Unfortunately, the bar temporarily closed in 2020 due to the Covid-19 pandemic and at the time of writing its fate remains unknown. But know this: the Admiral Duncan has survived worse. Undoubtedly, this ship will sail again.

THE APPLE TREE
45 Mount Pleasant, WC1X 0AE
theappletreelondon.com
Nearest Tube: Russell Square

You can count the number of LGBTQ+ bars that have opened in London over the last five years on two hands, and The Apple Tree is among them. Housed in a building dating back to the 1720s, this pub, hidden away between Farringdon and King's Cross, exemplifies how the city's queer scene has diversified. Along with providing LGBTQ+ folk with somewhere to booze, The Apple Tree also serves as a venue and community space with open mics, drag shows, theatre and a plethora of workshops and events on offer.

Like other more modern queer pubs and bars, there is an emphasis on inclusivity. This isn't another pub or bar catering solely to cisgender gay men; it offers a safe space for people of all sexualities and gender identities. The toilets are unisex (as they should be) and the bar staff are friendly, willing to reserve areas for you if you ask. Its proximity to Farringdon means that you might encounter straight men in suits picking up an after-work pint, but according to the owners, Lucy Fenton and Phil Hunt, the crowd is usually 80% LGBTQ+.

Inside, the pub has a charming higgledy-piggledy-but-make-it-glamorous approach to décor. It's loosely separated into a front and back, with high tables at the rear and more comfortable chairs and sofas in the main bar area. A large selection of vegan dishes are available from the kitchen, with some non-vegan options too. The drinks are surprisingly good value, considering the location. You can even indulge in alcoholic and non-alcoholic cocktails, although be warned that ordering something complicated on a Saturday night will make you unpopular with your fellow patrons. Upstairs is a function room, which doubles as a dressing room for events.

Fenton and Hunt also own the freehold of the building, and they told *Vice* that profits from the venue 'will continue to be ploughed back into the business and the community' – meaning that, hopefully, The Apple Tree will resist the constant threat of closure faced by so many of London's LGBTQ+ spaces.

CIRCA
62 Frith St, Soho, W1D 3JN
circasoho.com
Nearest Tube: Tottenham Court Road

Opened in 2011, Circa immediately found its footing with gay men in their late-twenties and thirties who were tiring of nights in Ku Bar but hesitant to make the transition to Comptons. That demographic has stuck; punters at Circa lean towards the conspicuously well-groomed and image-conscious men who stroll around Soho's streets. It can be

quite relaxed, though, especially when you're sat on one of the leather sofas, or near the entrance. As you progress back towards the bar area, things get more swish, with high stools, mirrors and a DJ booth hidden behind a giant disco ball. The drinks are serviceable, and while there are cocktails you might be better off sticking to a vodka, soda and lime. The muscled and coiffed bar staff are efficient, but can be brusque with customers who don't embody Circa's target audience. During Pride, they host a huge party, which always sees large groups congregating outside the bar on Frith Street.

CITY OF QUEBEC
12 Old Quebec St, Marylebone, W1H 7AF
greeneking-pubs.co.uk/pubs/greater-london/city-of-quebec
Nearest Tube: Marble Arch

The City of Quebec is allegedly London's oldest LGBTQ+ venue. Opened around 1946 in the aftermath of World War II, the pub was originally popular with gay service men in the Royal Air Force – although it operated covertly, as homosexuality was illegal in the UK at the time. Queer venues began to pop up in the 1970s, after the partial decriminalisation of homosexuality in 1967. The Quebec went public(ish), although keeping it open has been a battle. In 2014, the Quebec was bought by Green King Pubs, who initially planned to modernise the pub and shift it away from its queer roots. Indeed, after a renovation in 2015, things did change, and while the pub remained peripherally LGBTQ+, the clientele began to straighten. Thankfully, while the pub is still owned by Green King, new management

13

THE ADMIRAL DUNCAN BOMBING

On Friday 30 April 1999 at 6:37pm, at the start of the Bank holiday weekend, a nail bomb exploded at the Admiral Duncan, killing three people and injuring more than 70 others. It was the third in a string of bombings that took place in London during April that year, specifically targeting Black, South Asian and LGBTQ+ people. The first explosion occurred in Electric Avenue, Brixton, injuring 48 people, while a second bomb, planted on Brick Lane in Shoreditch, East London, injured a further 13.

The bomb at the Admiral Duncan saw the first fatalities. The device was discovered by the pub's manager, Mark Taylor, who had noticed a suspicious looking bag. It exploded while he was investigating. Taylor, thankfully, survived. Speaking to the BBC about what happened a few weeks after the attack, Taylor said, 'One of the bar staff recognised a package. I said, "Look, I don't think this is a hoax. I think it's the real thing." I went back around to see what see what colour and make the bag was and *bang!* That was it.'

Taylor had to undergo a number of surgeries. He had burns all over his body. 'I must have been three feet away from it, I went straight down on it,' he said. 'I just thought, *that's it. I've gone. I'm dead.* Everything was just black.' He was helped out the pub to find the police outside.

The explosion was described as 'like a thunderclap' and as something out of a war film. Jonathan Cash, who wrote the play *The First Domino* based on his experience of the bombing, was, at the time, a classified ads manager for *Gay Times*. He told the publication in 2009 that he heard 'the loudest, most alien sound'.

'I don't know how long it went on – a couple of seconds, perhaps,' he said. 'Then the most enormous crunch of something structural and solid. I felt no pain, just terror. My eyes were ringing, my nose filled with sulphurous dust and, in the blink of an eye, I saw unrecognisable shapes flying past towards the doors. With the dust and smoke, I could see little more than six inches in front of me. Somehow, I was on the floor. Then I heard the screaming. I didn't make any sound. Or perhaps I did. I can't remember.'

Two gay men, Nik Moore and John Light, and their pregnant straight friend, Andrea Dykes, died. They were having a drink before heading to see *Mamma Mia* in the West End. Dykes's husband, Julian, ended up in a coma for three weeks.

Within hours of the blast, which blew off most of the pub's entrance, 22-year-old David Copeland, an engineer's assistant on the London Underground, was arrested at his home in Cove, Hampshire. Copeland had ties to the far-right British National Party and was a member of the National Socialist Movement, a neo-Nazi group. He told police he acted alone and that his 'intent was to spread fear, resentment and hatred throughout this country; it was to cause a racial war'. On 30 June 2000, he was convicted of three counts of murder and of planting bombs, and given six concurrent life sentences.

On Monday 3 May 1999, thousands of people gathered for a vigil to pay tribute to the victims, with the London Gay Men's Chorus leading a procession from outside the Admiral Duncan, down Old Compton Street and up to Soho Square. The following Friday, hundreds gathered around the venue to pay their respects, with a service of remembrance held at nearby St Anne's Church, which rang its bell three times in memory of Andrea Dykes, John Light and Nik Moore.

Speaking ahead of the service, LGBTQ+ activist Peter Tatchell, then a spokesperson for Outrage!, a British queer rights group, said, 'As well as commemorating the bomb victims, we want to show our defiance of racism, homophobia and neo-Nazism. This vigil is a signal to all hate-mongers that our communities will not be divided or driven underground.'

On 13 June 2016, following the mass-shooting at Pulse in Orlando, Florida, which left 49 people dead and 53 injured, thousands gathered outside of the Admiral Duncan in solidarity with the victims and anyone affected.

At 7pm, there was a minute's silence before 49 balloons were released, and the London Gay Men's Chorus sang Simon & Garfunkel's 'Bridge Over Troubled Water'.

In 2019, a vigil was held outside of a rainbow flag-adorned Admiral Duncan to mark the 20th anniversary of the bombing. Around the corner in St Anne's Gardens you can find the Admiral Duncan Memorial Bench, designed by artist Simon Kidd, and three trees planted in memory of Andrea Dykes, John Light and Nik Moore.

A plaque honouring the memory of the three victims of the bombing.

re-diversified the events programme in 2019. While the pub's legendary karaoke nights from the '80s and '90s are no longer on the menu, there are a number of cabaret performances, drag shows, quizzes and club nights. What hasn't changed is the pub's reputation. The City of Quebec has always been popular with older gay gentlemen, garnering it a couple of nicknames, including 'The Elephant's Graveyard' and 'The Pacemaker's Arms'. It brings in a more mixed crowd nowadays, although it's still densely populated by mature men and their admirers.

COMPTONS
51-53 Old Compton St, Soho, W1D 6HN
comptonsofsoho.co.uk
Nearest Tube: Tottenham Court Road

Comptons has been a fixture on Old Compton Street for nearly 35 years. Before G-A-Y, Ku Bar and even the Admiral Duncan transformed Soho into London's gay district, this longstanding pub provided queer Londoners with a watering hole in the city centre. The windows were blacked out, as was the norm for gay establishments in the '80s, and the bar was quite small. Unlike West London spot the Coleherne Arms, Comptons was open to both lesbians and gay men, and was known for being 'friendly and traditional'. That hasn't changed, although the pub is somewhat larger today, and can lean a little masculine.

The four large front-facing windows, no longer blacked out, provide a glimpse into the circular ground floor bar, which is packed with men no matter the day of the week. The crowd is more mature than some Soho haunts, and if you like your beer with a side of butch queen you'll feel right at home (you can even occasionally find live rugby and football matches playing on the pub's TV screens). Comptons has a

reputation for being cruisy, so expect to find bearded blokes casting their eyes around the room, looking for their next meal. Upstairs in the lounge, things are more subdued, and if you get down early enough to grab yourself a table it can be a great spot to meet friends or a date. The drinks are typical central London prices (expect to pay around five quid for a pint) while the decor – all wood panelling, wallpaper and the occasional chandelier – emphasises the venue's old-school charm. She might be an oldie, but she's still a goodie; no wonder she's been dubbed the Grand Dame of Soho.

THE DUKE OF WELLINGTON
77 Wardour St, Soho, W1D 6QA
dukeofwellingtonsoho.co.uk
Nearest Tube: Tottenham Court Road

Not many spots in Soho offer a bit of both worlds. While Comptons has its calmer lounge bar, and Little Ku can provide some respite from the packed bodies at G-A-Y during the week, the Duke of Wellington is the area's true 'vers' queen. While it's definitely still a pub, the ground floor gives off big regional gay bar energy. The floor is sticky and there's little to no seating. Men huddle in groups, all pushed tightly against each other. The music isn't overly loud, although shuffling to whichever pop song is playing isn't frowned upon. Upstairs, however, things are more traditional. The bar on the first floor means you don't have to traipse up and down the precariously small spiral staircase every time you want a drink, and there's a bounty of seating, including corner areas where one can skulk off to with a date. Decor-wise, expect lots of wood – but unlike your usual boozer, it's accented with gold-patterned wallpaper. There's also a stellar pub quiz, which can be lawless and brilliantly chaotic (bookings are essential). Regular drinks offers keep the prices competitive – on certain nights you can pick up a pint for under three quid!

But what really sets this place apart is how friendly it is. While Soho is often associated with bitchiness, perhaps a by-product of how homogenous and commercialised it has become, the Welly welcomes everyone. The staff must be some of the nicest and most patient in all of W1D, and as a result you'll find a surprisingly mixed crowd, although it skews a little older. However, this is still Soho: expect to see more men than women and the obligatory bewildered tourists, who stumbled in expecting to find the classic British pub experience only to be accosted by a drag queen forcing people to lip sync to *Frozen's* 'Let It Go'.

FREEDOM BAR
60-66 Wardour St, Soho, W1F 0TA
freedombarsoho.com
Nearest Tube: Piccadilly Circus

Described by London queer-scene bible *QX* magazine as 'polysexual', Freedom Bar is only really an LGBTQ+ venue due to its proximity to Old Compton Street. Though the venue isn't explicitly queer, it caters to both a heterosexual and LGBTQ+ crowd, booking drag performers and comedians, and hosting cabaret and retro '50s, '60s and '70s nights. Recently refurbished, the place is tasteful inside, with sleek lighting and plenty of banquette seating. The bar prices reflect this: a cocktail will easily set you back a tenner, while a glass of house wine is around £6. Nevertheless, the downstairs 'club' does fill up on the weekend. Just remember: it's definitely a mixed crowd, so don't be surprised if things are more girls and their guy friends than gays with their gal pals.

THE FRIENDLY SOCIETY
79 Wardour St, Soho, W1D 6QB
Nearest Tube: Piccadilly Circus

There aren't too many basement bars left in Soho (RIP Madame JoJo's), especially basement bars that give you that thrilling clandestine feeling. But turn off Wardour Street and slip into the alleyway leading to Tisbury Court and you'll find the entrance to The Friendly Society, a subterranean Soho oddity keeping the area's freak flag flying. Descend the stairs and you'll enter a drinking den indebted to camp and kitsch. An army of Barbies and Action Men hang from the ceiling, while old movies are projected on the walls. The toilets are lit up with neon lights, as is the bar (which does offer cocktails, although ordering one might make you unpopular with the bar staff). While not explicitly a queer venue, you won't find anything heteronormative here. The Friendly Society entices a broad clientele of different orientations and gender identities, something Soho could do with a bit more of.

G-A-Y BAR
30 Old Compton St, Soho, W1D 4UR
g-a-y.co.uk
Nearest Tube: Tottenham Court Road

Opened in 2002, G-A-Y Bar is the flagship outpost of Jeremy Joseph's nightlife empire and has become a rite of passage for almost all LGBTQ+ people desperate for a first taste of London's infamous gay scene. With its gaping purple entrance and large silver signage, cheap drinks and dedication to blasting Top 40 hits both past and present, this three-floored behemoth is a playground for London's young queer things. Think of it as the student union

A stalwart resident of Old Compton Street, this pub has catered to the LGBTQ+ community for over 35 years.

bar of the capital's LGBTQ+ scene: all sticky floors and affable if slightly grumpy bar staff. Not that such an atmosphere puts off any Londoners aged over 25, many of whom moan about the place but can't resist the allure of cheap pints and pop music. For this reason, no matter the day of the week, the place is always packed. Weekday drinks offers are particularly good and the upstairs bar, with its dingy smoking area, makeshift dance floor and banks of wooden seating, fills up fast. The basement houses a dedicated girls' room for lesbians and queer womxn, while the cavernous ground floor has banquette seating at the rear and a nook for those seeking somewhere a little more intimate – not that it offers any privacy whatsoever (although that may be the point). Adorning the walls are innumerable screens playing music videos from icons such as Britney, Ariana and Beyoncé, giving the whole place an almost garish luminescence. It's a gaudy funhouse stuffed full of nearly every gay bar trope you could hope for.

HALFWAY II HEAVEN
7 Duncannon St, Charing Cross, WC2N 4JF
halfway2heaven.net/london
Nearest Tube: Charing Cross

Just a hop, skip and strut away from Trafalgar Square, Halfway II Heaven – so named because it sits roughly halfway between Soho and Heaven nightclub – may look like a traditional old-school boozer, but it's as fun and frivolous as gay bars come. Known for drawing an older but not necessarily more sophisticated crowd, the pub is surprisingly good value for money considering its central location. The main bar area isn't big, but there are standing tables for people to balance drinks on and enough room for small groups. If you're

lucky, you might even grab yourself a table at the back of the bar. Downstairs, the walls are covered in glitter and, depending on the night, you'll likely find a drag queen tottering around with a microphone, or someone doing karaoke or cabaret. Sometimes there's a DJ, if you want to get your groove on before rushing down to G-A-Y at Heaven, and things might get cruisy later in the night. It can be riotous, but that's no bad thing.

THE KING'S ARMS
23 Poland St, Soho, W1F 8QJ
kingsarms-soho.co.uk/london
Nearest Tube: Oxford Circus

The King's Arms has been a Soho fixture for nearly 40 years. In the '80s, the pub drew a more mixed crowd during the day, while evenings were strictly gay and popular with the so-called 'clones': muscled and moustachioed gay men who adopted the hypermasculine, mainstream look of the era (think lots of denim and flannel). It's likely that some of those clones – now older, perhaps broader and more mature, but still moustachioed – still frequent the King's Arms, which is why the pub is now known for its popularity with London's bear community: larger, heavy-set and hairy gay men. Inside, it's fairly traditional pub fare with lots of wooden panelling and, for central London, fairly ample seating, including a plush upstairs lounge that hosts private functions.

Atmosphere is important for a pub, and the King's Arms maintains a cosy one, although playfulness is definitely encouraged. On Friday and Saturday, DJs spin tunes, and if there's a 'big match' on you might catch the footie. A weekly quiz draws a large crowd, too. The slight distance from Old Compton Street doesn't prevent footfall, and space in the King's Arms can get tight, especially given its title as 'London's favourite bear bar' (the only bear bar, for what it's worth). But there's hardly ever attitude when the pub is packed; people are more than willing to share their space, and even tables, should you be so bold. The distance from the main LGBTQ+ strip also helps on the day of Pride, when Old Compton Street and its tributaries become intolerably busy. The King's Arms provides a little respite from the main march thoroughfare, but it's just as much fun, especially when they blast music out the windows for the crowd who always congregate outside. It might not be the obvious Soho choice, but the King's Arms is one of the area's crowning jewels. Owing to the COVID-19 pandemic, the King's Arms temporarily closed in 2020. Sadly, at the time of writing it remains uncertain whether it will reopen.

KU BAR
30 Lisle Street, Soho, WC2H 7BA
ku-bar.co.uk
Nearest Tube: Leicester Square

Originally opened in 1995 and taking its name from the legendary and now shuttered Ibiza spot, Ku Club; Ku Bar is an ongoing Soho success story. While gentrification, rising business rates and redevelopment have irrevocably altered London's entertainment district, Ku has managed to maintain itself, even flourish. Originally located on Charing Cross Road, the bar moved to Lisle Street in 2007 where owner, Gary Henshaw, started targeting a younger crowd seeking out alternatives to G-A-Y and Village Soho.

Another old dame of Soho, the King's Arms is London's favourite bear bar.

The flagship of a flourishing enterprise, Ku caters to partygoers seven days a week.

SHE - the only lesbian bar in London, tucked beneath Little Ku.

The venue, which is sometimes dubbed Ku Leicester Square, spreads over two floors: a ground-floor bar, which spills onto the streets during summer; and a compact basement space known as Klub.

Open seven days a week, you're always likely to find people at the bar, and even the basement can fill up on a Wednesday night. On Friday and Saturday, expect a queue to get into the basement. It can get so busy that if you're not good with tight, enclosed spaces you might want to give it a miss. Those who aren't bothered by sweaty bodies will find a small dance floor and a narrow bar, manned by good-looking, muscular men who, depending on the night, may or may not be shirtless. The music is your standard gay bar fare, with screens upstairs showing music videos interspersed with clips of hunky men. Henshaw also runs a bar on the first floor, above Ku. The Light Lounge is a separate, more upmarket cocktail bar that offers something quieter: ideal if you're looking to book a private function.

LITTLE KU
25 Frith Street, Soho, WC2H 7BA
ku-bar.co.uk
Nearest Tube: Tottenham Court Road

Little Ku can be found just north of Shaftesbury Avenue. This slender, two-story bar is described as the 'Ku Group's naughty sibling', although it's really just a condensed version of the flagship Leicester Square bar. The pop songs are the same, as are the music videos playing from a number of televisions on the wall, but given the size things feel a bit more intimate. There isn't much seating around the bar on the ground floor, but if you head upstairs you can take your pick of high tables with stools. The tables by the front windows offer a great view of Soho

– always entertaining for people-watchers – and on a weeknight you won't have a problem finding somewhere to sit. Just don't expect the same on a Friday or Saturday. This is prime Soho real estate, so come the weekend there's bound to be gaggles of gays eager to get the drinks in before heading to the basement club at Ku Bar or a night at Heaven.

RETRO BAR
2 George Ct, Charing Cross, WC2N 6HH
retrobarlondon.co.uk/london
Nearest Tube: Charing Cross

If you've ever heard someone decry that Old Compton Street is 'too commercial' (guilty as charged) then it's likely their favourite central London haunt is Retro Bar. While it's owned by Stonegate Pubs, a company that operates a large handful of gay pubs in the heart of the city, it escapes the accusations of conformity levelled at Soho. This is in part because of its music policy, which doesn't cater to Top 40 bops and House remixes. Retro Bar instead flirts with alternative music, indie, metal and the back-catalogues of rock and pop legends, many of whose faces adorn the bar walls (think Bowie and Beth Ditto, Iggy Pop and Debbie Harry). But it's also because, unlike many of its contemporaries, Retro really is open to the entire LGBTQ+ community. This is a queer pub, not a gay bar. The bar staff is made up of a variety of people from different sexualities and gender identities, and their events programming comprises of regular nights for trans people, and for lesbians and queer womxn. There's also their weekly quiz, hosted by London nightlife legend Princess Julia, which is always a hoot. In 2020, Retro Bar was temporarily closed because of the Covid-19 pandemic. At the time of writing it remains unclear if this beloved establishment will reopen its doors.

A POTTED HISTORY OF SOHO

Soho and the West End have long been epicentres of queer activity. During the 1600s and 1700s, the area had a reputation as a place where men would solicit other men for sex, although areas of the City of London, such as Bishopsgate and St. Paul's, were much more popular. By the beginning of the 19th century, Soho had become destitute and overcrowded. In the late 1880s, the West End underwent some regeneration: Piccadilly Circus was expanded, and theatres and music halls sprung up around Shaftesbury Avenue. With this entertainment district came a rise in sex work, and Soho soon nabbed itself the moniker 'the Meat Rack'. According to Historic England, a man named Jack Saul even roamed the roads, handing out cards advertising an all-male brothel on Cleveland Street.

The theatres in the area became hook-up spots, particularly the London Pavilion, a musical hall that later became a part of the London Trocadero shopping centre (and which now, rather fittingly, houses BODY WORLDS: an exhibition of human bodies, preserved through plastination). During the 1895 trials of Oscar Wilde, it became clear that the writer frequented the area, kissing waiters at the Soho restaurant Kettner's (recently re-opened) and hosting orgies at the Savoy Hotel. Just two years before the beginning of the First World War, the Cave of the Golden Calf opened below a draper's on Heddon Street. This cabaret and avant-garde-performance club, described as 'a place given up to gaiety', was for all intents and purposes the first 'gay bar', as we would understand it today. Like so many that followed, the Cave didn't last long, going bankrupt in 1914.

In 1896, the Trocadero Long Bar opened on the corner of Shaftesbury Avenue and Piccadilly Circus. It didn't take long before this gentlemen-only establishment became a renowned spot for homosexual liaisons, although it had a mixed crowd, catering to civil servants and queer men alike. In the 1920s, populist publication John Bull, a Sunday periodical, exposed 'six notorious places' that it had dubbed 'bogus hotels': spots of alleged disrepute that were said to house fornicators, prostitutes and sodomites. Among these six places was the Hotel de France on Villiers Street, where legendary LGBTQ+ nightclub Heaven now sits.

By the 1930s, however, Soho had a thriving club scene, and was popular with those who committed so-called 'immoral activity'. Most famous of these venues is the Caravan Club, described as 'London's greatest bohemian rendezvous'. This private members' club in the basement of 81 Endell Street was owned by Jack Neave and William Reynolds, and for the handsome price of one shilling (or six if you weren't a member), guests could expect 'all-night gaiety'. According to police files, the venue was under constant surveillance, and in 1934 undercover officers raided the venue. Describing the club, raid leader Detective Inspector Clarence Campion noted that he saw people 'acting in a very obscene manner'. 'Men were dancing with men and women with women, a number of couples were simply standing still,' he said in a report. 'I saw couples wriggling their posteriors, and where I saw men together, they had their hands on the other's buttocks and were pressing themselves together.' The venue closed in 1934.

Still, it wasn't the only queer club in the area. The Shim Sham Club, which opened on Wardour Street in the mid-1930s, was described as 'London's miniature Harlem'. Central to the Black jazz scene at the time, and closely linked with African American culture, the spot operated without a license, hosting what were then known as 'bottle parties'. While music was central to the club's DNA, it was also a space for politics and anti-fascist meetings, welcoming people of all races and sexualities. Letters sent to police at the time describe the space as a 'rendezvous for homosexual perverts', with interracial mingling and relationships similarly chastised. One letter states that the club's 'encouraging of Black and White intercourse [was] the talk of the West End'. In 1935, the club was shut down following a police raid, only to re-open as the Rainbow Roof, a similar venue that was charged with unlicensed dancing and music in 1936. It later became the Flamingo Club.

While none of these queer establishments operated openly, they were known to Londoners. The Second World War pushed queer culture further underground, although a number of bars and clubs popped up during the '40s – including the City of Quebec, which still functions today. Likewise, in 1968, legendary cabaret and burlesque club Madame Jojo's opened. Still, the West End and Soho had fallen out of favour with the city's queers, who had started to venture into West London, especially Earl's Court, where rents and accommodation was cheaper.

It wasn't until the 1980s that Soho flourished again, becoming the LGBTQ+ wonderland it is today. The Sundown Club in the basement of the Astoria on Charing Cross Road began hosting Bang! in 1976, and Heaven opened in 1979. Soho also became London's red-light district; it was filled with sex shops and brothels, some of which still linger. Nevertheless, by 1987 Westminster Council had clamped down. The sex industry in the area diminished exponentially, leaving numerous empty premises. In 1986, a pub called the Swiss Tavern, which had a reputation for being popular with gay men, became an explicitly queer venue, Comptons. Soon after, the Village, Halfway II Heaven, Rupert Street and the Yard all opened. The 1999 bombing of the Admiral Duncan only cemented Soho's queer legacy, proving that in the face of hatred and persecution, the LGBTQ+ community of London had found its home.

Like many areas of London, Soho hasn't been immune to gentrification and redevelopment. Crossrail in particular hit the area hard, with LGBTQ+ spaces such as the Ghetto, queer café First Out and the Astoria all demolished to make way for the new Elizabeth Line. Similarly, property developers have snapped up much of the area, transforming lots into luxury flats or chain shops. In 2014, Madame Jojo's was forced to close after a violent incident saw the council revoke the venue's license. However, the swiftness of the council's decision led many to speculate that the true motivator was gentrification. Queer pub Molly Moggs also closed, only to re-open briefly as a gay cocktail bar. It is now just a generic pub. Similarly, Man Bar, Shadow Lounge and the Green Carnation have all closed.

There is a note of hope. While undoubtedly, COVID-19 will stamp its impact on queer spaces, it was announced in 2019 that Madame Jojo's, which has sat empty since its closure, would re-open as a burlesque and cabaret venue. Likewise, the Ku Group recently opened She bar after the only other lesbian bar in London, Candy Bar, closed. These might seem like small wins – but as history shows, Soho has withstood numerous attempts at gentrification and redevelopment, as well as bombs, police raids and even the cholera outbreak of 1854. London's LGBTQ+ community won't give up their grip on Soho without a fight.

London's present collides with its past, in Soho Square.

RUPERT STREET BAR
50 Rupert St, Soho, W1D 6DR
rupert-street.com/london
Nearest Tube: Tottenham Court Road

If your idea of a night out involves ogling muscled bar staff in tight fitting tank tops, Rupert Street Bar, colloquially known as Rupert's, is the spot for you. Definitely a 'bar' rather than a 'pub', the emphasis here is on quickie cocktails and large goblets of pink gin, soundtracked to pop hits and House remixes. It's cruisy, especially if you're into the suited and booted after-work type, although later on Friday and Saturday nights the clientele gets pretty mixed. There are aspirations of sophistication, but the garish interiors aren't as chic as they perhaps hoped. Still, expect decent drinks offers before 8pm, and a quiet little nook at the back that's perfect for a night out with the gays and gals. Any cheesy gay bar decor can be forgiven.

SHE SOHO
23a Old Compton St, Soho, W1D 5JL
ku-bar.co.uk
Nearest Tube: Tottenham Court Road

It's symptomatic of a wider issue that She is the only dedicated lesbian bar in London. Over the past two decades, much of the city's LGBTQ+ scene has eroded away, weathered by modern developments, gentrification, rising business rates, unaffordable rents and a global recession. There was always a dearth of spaces explicitly for lesbians and queer womxn, but over 20 years these have been all but eradicated. It's not just London; there has been a global shrinkage in the number of lesbian bars, even in cities like New York and San Francisco. Along with the other forces trampling on LGBTQ+

spaces, societal inequalities mean women, especially queer women of colour, often have less disposable income and less political or cultural capital than queer cisgender men. Decades of marketing towards gay men created an infrastructure that has traditionally excluded lesbians and queer women, and thus there is a rich history of alternative, community-led spaces. As famed illustrator and activist Alison Bechdel once said, 'Lesbians are inherently uncommodifiable.'

That hasn't stopped the Ku Group's Gary Henshaw from trying. After he bought the famous lesbian spot, Candy Bar, in 2011, a 50% increase in rents forced the venue to close three years later. Soon after, the Ku Group launched She Soho, a bunker-like basement bar below Little Ku. With its own entrance, this tunnel-like bar only offers space for around 80 people. While it isn't women only, it is women first, and men are only really permitted when accompanying women and non-binary folk as their guests. The interior is sleek and modern, having undergone a refit in 2017, with benched seating at one end and a bar at the other. There are a number of themed nights including quizzes, karaoke, cabaret and Open Box, a drag king talent competition. Tuesday nights are often busy as people pre-game at She before heading to the womxn's night at Klub (Ku Bar), while on the weekends, thanks to its proximity to Old Compton Street, you can expect the place to be rammed with Soho revellers.

VILLAGE SOHO
81 Wardour St, Soho, W1D 6QD
villagesoho.co.uk/london-bar
Nearest Tube: Tottenham Court

Originally a bar on Hanway Place, just off Tottenham Court Road, Village Bar led the charge of new LGBTQ+ locales into central London. Opened in the early '90s, it was notable for its (then) modern decor and, most importantly, its windows, which – unlike so many other queer venues in the city – weren't blacked out. The bar proved so popular that sibling franchises, Village Soho on Wardour Street and The Yard, were launched a year or so later. Shortly after that, however, the original Village Bar closed, and over the years Village Soho fell out of favour. Today though, the place is buzzing. Very much living up to your stereotypical idea of a 'gay bar', the place pumps out Janet Jackson and Rihanna while shirtless gogo boys, a rarity on London's LGBTQ+ scene, dance on poles. Recently refurbished, the place has become more inclusive, removing all gendered restrictions from the bathrooms, and, for Soho, the crowd is somewhat eclectic. As a result, it can fill up fast in the evenings, especially on the weekends. You might be able to find seating in the quieter upstairs lounge (great for people-watching, if you nab a spot by a window). Village Soho isn't subtle. But it is sexy, and there's nothing wrong with that.

THE YARD
57 Rupert St, Soho, W1D 7PL
yardbar.co.uk
Nearest Tube: Tottenham Court Road

Opened in 1992, The Yard is a Soho staple. One of the only gay bars in the area to promise outdoor space, you should aim to arrive early enough to secure a table in its little courtyard. There's greenery and plants, and the entryway is flanked by wiry trees. On a warm evening, this can be a real treat. However, if you're not one of the lucky ones, things get cramped quickly. If you're stood outside, expect to get jostled as people manoeuvre the tight space. The ground floor is usually packed with people queuing for drinks, and while there is seating, the number of

bodies crowding the bar gives the space a frantic quality. Upstairs in the Loft Bar, which can be booked for private functions, things are a smidge calmer. There's better seating and a small terrace, perfect for smokers and those wanting to watch groups mingle in the courtyard. Food is available – if you're brave – but really, The Yard is a place for gossiping over a beer or a bottle (or two) of wine.

SINK THE PINK

Sink The Pink have been 'queering the norm' with their outrageous parties, fabulous performances and genderfuck antics since 2008. Founded by best friends Glyn Fussell and Amy Redmond in response to the lack of truly inclusive and exciting nights out in London, the night has grown from its cult beginnings at the Bethnal Green Working Men's Club to selling out shows at London's Troxy, Roundhouse and Brixton Academy.

Those initial nights in East London were chaotic, anarchic and insane amounts of fun. Featuring performances from drag artists, heady pop tunes and a crowd of people dressed in all manner of spangled outfits, Sink the Pink regularly maxed out capacity, providing the city's misfits with a space where they could explore their gender identities and sexualities through unbounded self-expression. The move to the Troxy turbo-boosted their goals, offering bigger performances, guest sets from pop legends and a truly bacchanalian queer fantasy.

Sink The Pink is more than just a legendary club night. Over the years, they've become a collective melting pot of creatives, artists, choreographers, performers and designers, whose skills and talent have diversified the STP programme. Sink the Pink now offers annual pantomimes, festival appearances and their 'Sink The Pink Street Party', a day-long jamboree of queer artists, popstars and drag in Finsbury Park. Sink The Pink even has its own spin offs, like cult dance party Savage Disco, which ran at Metropolis Strip Club between 2014 and 2019, and Mighty Hoopla, a 25,000 capacity festival dedicated to pop music and LGBTQ+ inclusivity.

The Sink The Pink team have performed all around the world, from Sao Paolo to New York, and worked with brands like Hunter and YSL. They've collaborated with popstars such as Years & Years, Little Mix and actual Spice Girl Mel C, who went on tour with the collective's drag performers in 2019. Sassy, fierce and fabulous, Sink The Pink have changed queer London for the better.

CLUBS

CIRCA THE CLUB
Hungerford House, Victoria Embankment,
Charing Cross, WC2N 6PA
circatheclub.com
Nearest Tube: Embankment

A newcomer to the capital's queer clubbing scene, and one of the first permanent LGBTQ+ clubs to open in central London in over 15 years, Circa the Club, run by the team behind Circa the Bar on Frith Street, takes the DNA of its namesake and supersizes it. With space for 750 people and a 4am license, it's a great alternative to nearby superclub Heaven, even if the drinks are still wildly expensive. The space, which used to be a naff bar called Opal and, at one point, an Australian pub, has been renovated and reimagined, and it's quite impressive. Exposed brick, tasteful lighting and (of course) disco balls are the vibe, while the tunes are your typical souped-up house music. While everyone is welcome, Circa the Club is skewed towards gay men; this is the sort of club where muscled men take their tops off after midnight. It draws a similar crowd to its sister bar, so expect everyone to look groomed and put together, even if all they're wearing is a Speedo and a harness. It's cruisy and sexy and the perfect spot if you're on the prowl.

Circa the Club is one of the latest supersize clubs to enter London's queer nightlife scene.

G-A-Y LATE

5 Goslett Yard, Soho, WC2H 0EA
g-a-y.co.uk
Nearest Tube: Tottenham Court Road

This late-night iteration of Jeremy Joseph's G-A-Y franchise isn't as polished or glossy as the big nights at Heaven or the flagship bar around the corner. Perhaps it's the late license – G-A-Y Late is open until 3am seven days a week. Or maybe it's just because the venue is tucked down a side street between a Starbucks and the Tottenham Court Road Station redevelopment. Either way, there's a thrilling, almost clandestine feeling as you swoop around the corner from Charing Cross Road into Goslett Yard and make your way inside (if you can get past the door staff, who aren't known for their friendliness).

It's the sort of place you don't plan on visiting, but find yourself scurrying to when after-work drinks in Soho escalate. It's fairly compact: spread over one floor with two sunken seating areas at either side of the venue, a curved bar that services the whole space and a few raised platforms, usually complete with a number of dancing gays. Like G-A-Y Bar, the walls are covered in large televisions playing pop music videos, and there's the typical sticky floors, less-than-pleasant bathroom, wooden seating and insanely cheap drinks offers during the week. It's rough around the edges and lacks any attempts of grandeur, but at 2am when you want to stretch out your night a little longer by dancing to Lady Gaga while sipping inexpensive vodka, lime and sodas, there's no better place to let your recklessness run wild.

G-A-Y @ HEAVEN

The Arches, Villiers St, WC2N 6NG
g-a-y.co.uk
Nearest Tube: Charing Cross/Embankment

G-A-Y at Heaven is humongous. No matter when you go, you're bound to lose your friends – until you bump into them on the dance floor an hour later. Spread over two floors with four different rooms, each section offers a different soundtrack for your night. In the main room, you'll find Top 40 hits and House remixes of Cheryl Cole songs. The straight-up pop room is tucked away through some doors and around the corner, spinning nostalgic hits from the '80s and '90s. Then there's what was once called 'the Departure Lounge', a sort of VIP space that offers karaoke on busier nights. Upstairs, you'll find the R&B/Hip Hop room, arguably the most raucous and fun space in the venue.

Like Joseph's other establishments, the price of drinks varies depending on which night of the week you visit, and the bathrooms leave something to be desired. The crowd also skews younger, although on Saturday nights you won't feel out of place if you're over 26. You can usually pick up a flyer for reduced entry from outside G-A-Y Bar – which results in a bunch of queers racing down Charing Cross Road and through Trafalgar Square in a bid to save a couple of quid before the offer runs out at midnight. On a Saturday night you might see a popstar performing live, with Miley Cyrus, Kylie Minogue and The Pussycat Dolls all having made an appearance in the last decade.

The city's most (in)famous gay club.

G·A·Y

Maximum Of 6 People Per Tab

G-A-Y

There has been a version of G-A-Y in London for 45 years, although it hasn't always gone by that name. In the late '70s, promoters Norman Scott, Damien Tony and Jerry Collins, launched Bang at Sundown, the basement venue at the Astoria, a former theatre, cinema and ballroom on Charing Cross Road. Collins, who went by the DJ name Gary London, was inspired by the Los Angeles club Studio One (now called the Factory) and Bang lived up to its Californian aspirations. 'Walking into Bang's a bit like walking into a Hollywood musical,' wrote one journalist for *Capital Gay*, a free weekly gay newspaper published in London between 1981 and 1995. 'The illusion of movies continues inside... a quick right turn brings you onto a huge circular balcony. Here you can look down on the dance floor over a glass and chrome balustrade. Those who prefer to watch, or just need a rest, lean over the rail, as over the side of a ship.'

While there had been other gay discos in London, Bang was, really, the first of its kind. Initially running on a Monday night – many gay discos were relegated to the quieter nights during the week – further events were organised for Thursday and, later, Saturday nights after a year of queues around the block, national press coverage and countless celebrity patrons such as Bowie and Rod Stewart.

In 1992, Bang was taken over by promoter and DJ Jeremy Joseph, who changed the name to G-A-Y, the name of a radio show he hosted. Joseph saw the opportunity to boost the night's profile by inviting pop acts to perform live at the club. In 1993, he clinched things and cemented G-A-Y's legacy when Kylie Minogue, already a gay icon, performed on the evening of Pride. For over a decade, G-A-Y at the Astoria would see megastars such as Madonna, Britney Spears and every solo Spice Girl perform. Geri 'Ginger Spice' Horner, née Halliwell, even wrote a song about partying there. 'G-A-Y was one of the first places I performed,' she told newspaper *The Guardian*. 'It left a massive impression on me. I love the atmosphere and the spirit of the people.' The draw of massive popstars, a rotation of Top 40 hits and the famous balloon drops meant that during the 2000s, G-A-Y became the biggest gay club in the UK.

Towards the end of the decade, the Astoria first found itself up for sale and then inconveniently placed for the development of Crossrail. Coincidentally, there was talk during this time that Heaven, dubbed 'the most famous gay nightclub in the world', also faced closure. G-A-Y had already expanded into two further venues. G-A-Y Bar on Old Compton Street and G-A-Y Late, and rumours circulated that Joseph had been eyeing Heaven as a possible alternative to the Astoria. After Heaven was saved, G-A-Y moved there on Friday 3 October 2008. Since then, Jeremy Joseph has taken full ownership of Heaven and launched an outpost of G-A-Y in Manchester. The spirit of the night, however, remains the same.

In 2016, Joseph was criticised for a racist post on social media blaming 'scum gangs, Somalians, drug deals' for an increase in violent crime in Soho. He later issued an apology, writing, 'The fact that some of these gangs are Somali is irrelevant and I should never have highlighted that fact, even in the heat of the moment which it was.' He added that he had reached out to 'work with members of the community, including UK Black Pride, in what we can do to increase diversity awareness within our community so that mistakes of the kind that I made are not repeated.'

For some LGBTQ+ Londoners, Joseph's comments – along with his establishment's highly commercialised nature, brusque door staff and history of excluding queer womxn – were the final nail in the coffin for G-A-Y. But London is an ever-growing organism, and as more people flock to the capital they can't resist the lure of the city's most (in)famous gay club. For many, an iconic name, a performance from a popstar and a night dancing to bangers still appeals.

VAULT 139
139-143 Whitfield Street Fitzrovia, W1T 5EN
vault139.com
Nearest Tube: Warren Street

Strictly men only, Vault 139 is one of London's last remaining cruise bars, offering unadulterated pleasure every day of the week (or at least between the hours of 1pm to 1am). Depending on the time of day and the day of the week, visitors will either be clothed and cruising, in their underwear, naked or, on Saturday nights, a combination of all three. Adult videos play on screens and there are plenty of corners for debauched deeds, including a number of backrooms. There is an entrance fee, but it gives you a lot of bang for your buck: not only will they look after your clothes if you plan on ditching your threads, but you also receive a free drink token (just remember to pick it up, as the people on the door can be forgetful) – and, for some reason, there's free WIFI. On certain days, to seduce the Grindr generation, under-25s get in free, but there's usually a steady stream of boys of all legal ages, shapes and sizes coming through the door. Regardless of the type of men and mischief you're into, you'll find something for you.

CLUB NIGHTS

DESI BOYZ
Great Portland St, W1W 5PN
desiboyz.co.uk
Nearest Tube: Regent's Park

Desi Boyz dubs itself as 'the busiest Desi LGBT night in the UK'. Founded in 2014, this monthly party takes place at 299 near Regent's Park, serving up the best bhangra, hip hop, R&B, Bollywood and House-fusion while providing LGBTQ+ Asians and their friends with a safe and welcoming space.

EXILIO LONDON LGBTQ LATIN DANCE CLUB
Bar & Co Boat, Temple Pier, Victoria
Embankment, WC2R 2PN
exilio.co.uk
Nearest Tube: Temple

Gloria Lizcano, a Columbian woman living in London, founded Exilio in 1996 after she became frustrated with the lack of nights out for the city's queer Latinx community. Now, 24 years later, Exilio, which translates as 'exile', is one of city's hidden treasures. You can dance to a mixture of salsa, merengue, bachata, reggaeton, cumbia, electro Latino and more. Even better: it all takes place on a boat. Or, to be more specific, a moored, pier-side barge reimagined as a bar. Right by Temple Tube station, it stays open until 3am.

HEAVEN IS A PLACE ON EARTH

In 1979, just 12 years after the partial decriminalisation of homosexuality, London welcomed the arrival of its first superclub. Heaven opened its doors in December at what used to be Global Village, a tatty roller-disco-cum-cinema under the arches of Charing Cross Station. Inspired by clubs like Pacha and New York's Paradise Garage, founder Jeremy Norman (who was also responsible for the Embassy club, itself a take on the infamous Studio 54) wanted to push London's gay nightlife scene out from the pub discos and basement bars and into the mainstream. Working with designer David Frost, Norman spent nearly £300,000 renovating the space. He brought Stephen Hayter from the Embassy club to manage things, who then tracked down and signed up Ian Levine as the resident DJ. Hayter soon left, replaced by David Inches, who would run the place for years. On opening night, the first song played was Dan Hartman's 'Relight My Fire'.

Heaven operated a fairly strict door policy. For a long time it was gay men only, especially on Saturday nights – although in her book, *Club Cultures: Boundaries, Identities and Otherness* (Routledge, 2009), Silvia Rief points out that the 'spatial setting' made policing this almost impossible. Indeed, Heaven was, and still is, ginormous. Spread across various levels and rooms, the club is a gay adventure playground, a warren of disco debauchery. When it opened, the cavernous main room, complete with balcony and stage, boasted impressive high-tech lighting and lasers, as well as a sound-system said to be based on one created for Elton John's concert tours. Still, in a write up for *The Evening Standard*, one reviewer echoed Rief's assertion: 'Heaven's biggest headache could be in deterring London's non-gay discophiles who could end up trying to pass for gay to get past the elegant bouncers at the disco's equivalent of the Pearly Gate.'

Nevertheless, Norman's insistence on a gay-male-only door policy was implemented for a reason. Heaven wasn't just a discotheque, but a space for gay men to safely cruise and even hook up. One of the various rooms partitioned off from the main room was The Cellar Bar, which had its own dedicated entrance. With a strict dress code of either leather, denim, rubber or boots depending on the night, this corner of Heaven required a membership. Members were issued with a key to gain entrance. Inside was an upstairs area and a small main room that housed the bar, and to the right were a number of dark corners and passages where men could slope off to have sex with one another. According to the writer Mark Langthorne, who worked behind the bar in 1983 and co-wrote the book *Somebody to Love* (Blink Publishing, 2016), it was a favourite haunt of Queen frontman Freddie Mercury, who would attempt to blend into the crowd by adopting the style of the time – a hypermasculine, moustachioed aesthetic that included form-fitting white t-shirts or vests, blue denim and leather, all inspired by uniforms – dubbed the 'clone look'.

In 1982, Heaven was sold to Richard Branson's Virgin Group, and by the mid '80s David Inches's managerial talents saw the club progressing and diversifying. 'Pyramid', a mixed night hosted on a Wednesday, was one of the first to start playing the house music that was beginning to make its way across the Atlantic from Chicago, while throughout the rest of the '80s and into the '90s Heaven became known as a proponent of Acid House, Techno and rave culture. The Cellar Bar closed in 1985, becoming The Altar and then Soundshaft, which would go on to host seminal House night 'Troll'. Like the Cellar Bar, 'Troll' was a favourite of famous faces, and the lack of a VIP area meant that clubbers might catch the likes of Grace Jones or Rupert Everett at the bar.

Heaven was still a gay venue though, and when 'Pyramid' ended it was replaced in the main club by 'Fruit Machine', a queer night hosted by drag queen The Fabulous Miss Kimberley that once played host to a performance from RuPaul, while Saturdays were reserved for 'Heaven is Saturday – Saturday is Heaven'. In 1998, the club underwent a refurb, introducing an indie night, 'Room Two', and 'Popcorn', a commercial night which still runs today and has become a favourite with students.

Nevertheless, after passing between various hands, Heaven found itself in a precarious state in 2013. Swooping in to save the venue from closure and potential redevelopment was G-A-Y founder, Jeremy Joseph, who took out a huge loan, using his own home and company as collateral, to rescue Heaven and the G-A-Y brand, which had moved to the venue a year prior.

Seven years later and both G-A-Y and Heaven are thriving. The venue always had a history of live music, with the likes of New Order, Culture Club, Sade, Sylvester and the Eurythmics playing club shows in the '80s and '90s. Over the past decade it has become one of London's most sought after gig venues, with Dua Lipa and Lily Allen doing full shows. Similarly, Joseph has continued G-A-Y's tradition of inviting huge pop divas to perform on Saturday clubnights, and it's not unusual to see the likes of Cher, Kylie Minogue and Lady Gaga grace the stage to perform to hundreds of sweaty, inebriated gays. Joseph recently gave the interior of Heaven another update, and it remains to this day one of the city's most technologically advanced superclubs, drawing LGBTQ+ folk and their allies from all over the country.

Of course, the music has become more commercial. Whereas before you might have stumbled upon a dark corner to find two men shagging, now you can get married in the venue. But the fact that Heaven still stands is emblematic of London's queer resilience. In a city with an almost untenable appetite for change no matter the cost, Heaven's perseverance is a beacon of strength. In 2020, the venue was made an 'Asset of Community Value', protecting it from property developers and cementing its legacy as an important LGBTQ+ space in the city. Perhaps Heaven really is holy after all.

The first queer superclub in London, Heaven has been sanctified as an 'Asset of community value'.

NORTH

BARS

THE BELL (BIG CHILL KING'S CROSS)
257-259 Pentonville Road , N1 9NL

The Bell was a queer pub in King's Cross on Pentonville Road, known for both partying and activism. Operating throughout the 1980s, the pub was one of the scene's more left-of-centre establishments, drawing groups like Lesbians and Gays Support the Miners and Lesbians Against Pit Closures. 'It was an amazing atmosphere,' Steve Rayner, a former bartender, told *The Guardian* in 2017. 'No one ever wanted to leave. Some nights we'd be open till three in the morning. Occasionally it got a bit rough, what with the women attacking one another with pool cues. I'd get in between them and then they'd start on me. In the end, we stopped putting the pool table out in the evenings.' Despite the fights, The Bell was more inclusive than most queer venues, welcoming to the entire LGBTQ+ community and not just gay men, unlike a lot of the bars at that time. It was also popular because it played more alternative music, like The Smiths, the Eurythmics, Siouxsie & the Banshees, The Associates, The Cult, the KLF and Kate Bush. 'The vibe at The Bell was democratic, egalitarian, accepting, colourful, idiosyncratic,' wrote Collin Clews for the website Gay in the '80s in 2017. 'Its effect was like alchemy, getting under the skin and changing people forever.' It is now The Big Chill bar.

THE BLACK CAP
171 Camden High St, Camden Town, NW1 7JY

Known as the 'Palladium of Drag', The Black Cap was a pub and cabaret venue in Camden. While licensing records date it back to the 1750s, this former boozer only became popular with the city's queer community in the mid-1960s, a number of years before the partial decriminalisation of homosexuality and the Stonewall Riots in New York. Those keen to see footage of the pub from this time should visit the BFI Mediatheque, where they can watch (for free) the 1969 film *Black Cap Drag*, which depicts two drag queens, Shane and Laurie Lee, performing and discussing their craft.

Many drag and cabaret performers got their start at The Black Cap. It was home to veteran performers like Mrs. Shufflewick (aka Rex Jameson), who the upstairs bar was named after, and Lily Savage. In more recent years, the venue saw performances from the queens of *RuPaul's Drag Race* and London favourites, like Lady Lloyd and Baga Chips, as well as club nights. However, it was starting to look threadbare.

The venue closed in 2015, despite its Asset of Community Value status protecting it from development. Since then, there have been a number of failed attempts by the owners to turn the first, second and third floor into flats, all of which have been rejected by Camden Council. During this time, community group We Are The Black Cap was formed to try and save the venue, and operate it as a not-for-profit venture.

CENTRAL STATION
37 Wharfdale Road, N1 9SD
centralstation.co.uk
Nearest Tube: King's Cross St. Pancras

Central Station is a King's Cross staple, having served the area for over 20 years. While the pub draws a wide clientele – you often spot students nursing drinks, which are affordable by London standards – it's still an LGBTQ+ watering hole. From the outside, you might expect a cosy and traditional interior. Step through the doors, however, and you'll be greeted with a ground floor that looks like a gay bar crossbred with a suburban leisure centre. Circular tables and wood chairs dot the floor, while the bar itself looks like a reception area. The walls are painted an optimistic purple, complemented by flamingo wallpaper. A room at the back houses a pool table, and upstairs you'll find a rare commodity: a terraced garden. On Monday and Friday nights expect haphazardly organised karaoke, while the weekends are dedicated to cabaret shows. If all that gets too much, or you can't be arsed to get an Uber home, Central Station is also a B&B (their cooked breakfast looks good, for what it's worth). It's not necessarily somewhere you'd pick as a destination, but make no mistakes: you'll have fun if you end up here.

ZODIAC BAR
114 Junction Road, N19 5LB
zodiacbar.london
Nearest Tube: Tufnell Park/Archway

Housed in what was once a Northern Soul bar, Zodiac opened in the summer of 2020. Beginning initially as a club night, Zodiac's mastermind, Jade (a transwoman who also goes by the name Lady Phoenix), took over the venue and transformed it into an inclusive LGBTQ+ space. With regular drag shows and plans to introduce fetish nights, they also host themed nights catering to bears, the trans community, and lesbians and queer womxn. Open Wednesday to Saturday, the bar boasts plenty of seating. Food is provided by a rotating crew from London's street food community, and there's a private room that can double as a dance floor as well as a soundproof karaoke room. There's even a secluded roof terrace. New queer venues crop up so rarely that Zodiac bar is a welcome addition to the scene.

The neon glow of a night out in London.

CLUBS

SCALA
275 Pentonville Rd, N1 9NL
scala.co.uk
Nearest Tube: King's Cross St. Pancras

Run as a cinema until 1993, the Scala mutated into a club and live music venue at the turn of the millennium. The venue hosted seminal queer club night Popstarz for almost eight years, where queer acts like Scissor Sisters and Le Tigre performed. Since then, the Scala has become one of London's most prestigious live music venues, home of Winter Pride UK. In 2019, Popstarz returned to the Scala for a one-off party to celebrate the venue's 20th anniversary.

THE UNDERGROUND CLUB
37 Wharfdale Road, N1 9SD
theundergroundclub.net
Nearest Tube: King's Cross St Pancras

In the basement of King's Cross hangout Central Station, you'll find a den for kinky kings and queens. The Underground Club touts itself as London's longest running Men Only club, although that title is a little misleading. While most of the club's nights are geared towards cruising and fetishes (Club Sop for piss play; Pants for underwear fans; Gearfreaxxx if you're into leather wear, sportswear, biker gear and so on; Club Spankz for spanking and corporal punishment), the Underground Club also hosts Sweet Wednesday, a party for the transgendered community that is open to transgirls and their admirers. While Sweet Wednesday has an X-rated reputation, there's a strong community among visitors. Those uncomfortable or unable to travel in their outfits can make use of the private changing facilities and make-up area, and if you're unsure of how to do anything – or just fancy a makeover – Pearl, Sweet Wednesday's in-house makeup girl, is on hand. Visitors on any given night have access to the bar upstairs at Central Station (although appropriate clothing is mandatory) and the terrace. You can also book a room at the B&B.

CLUB NIGHTS

ADONIS

facebook.com/adonispourhommelondon

adonis.eventcube.io

Club night

Usually hosted in a Tottenham warehouse, Adonis is the latest club night to take London's queer scene, chew it up, spit it out, then set it on fire. Pure, subversive hedonism, this underground queer party truly lives up to the adage: anything goes. While it draws a crowd of youngsters and creatives, there's nothing posy about it – it's completely cross-generational. People come here to let go, whether that means dancing for 18 hours straight to cutting-edge electronic music, sucking dick in the darkroom or just mingling with a diverse mix of LGBTQ+ people who are out to have a good time. If you're tired of hearing stories about how fabulous London's queer clubbing used to be, head to Adonis and experience that past glory for yourself.

POPSTARZ

popstarz.org

Popstarz was founded by the late promoter Simon Hobart in 1995 as the antithesis of London's hegemonic LGBTQ+ scene. Originally hosted at the now demolished Paradise club in Islington, the night eschewed the dance music and pop house that had come to dominate the city's gay scene, focusing on Britpop and indie. As the night jumped to bigger and better venues, its scope widened, filling multiple rooms that catered to pop fans (the songs always left of centre), electro lovers and R&B. During its eight-year stint at the Scala in King's Cross, Hobart and business partner Tommy Turntables, who would later run the infamous Ghetto in Soho, began booking alternative popstars, including the Scissor Sisters, Mika, Goldfrapp, Gossip and Calvin Harris.

In 2005, Hobart sadly passed away. Popstarz continued, moving to Soho and Holborn with festival slots and guest appearances, before finally landing in Vauxhall. But with the decline of the indie music scene and an increase in alternative LGBTQ+ nightlife in the city, as well as the difficulties of pre-Night Tube London, Turntables decided to end Popstarz. 'I didn't want Popstarz limping along, because to work, it needs to be a big, glorious event,' he told *Time Out*. 'So it felt like the right time to bow out.' In 2019, to celebrate the 20th anniversary of the Scala, Popstarz returned for a one-off party, which proved so popular that another one was planned for 2020. As their website reads: 'Stay tuned, there's plenty more to come!'

EAST

BARS

DALSTON SUPERSTORE
117 Kingsland High St, Dalston, E8 2PB
dalstonsuperstore.com
Nearest Tube: Dalston Kingsland Overground

Dalston Superstore isn't so much a bar as a lifestyle. It was opened in 2009 by Dan Beaumont, the man behind monthly cult Hi-NRG night Disco Bloodbath at the now shuttered Joiner's Arms; and Matt Tucker and Dan Hope, whose weekly Trailer Trash party was at On the Rocks (now Basing House in Shoreditch). Embodying alternative queer nightlife, the venue was, in Beaumont's words, 'achingly fashionable', drawing a crowd of artists and creatives who remain the bedrock of the venue's success. Superstore's parties separated it from the clubs and bars of Soho with lesbian nights, trans and non-binary nights, bisexual parties and events for queer people of colour.

That attitude has only solidified in the subsequent decade. Superstore now pulses at the heart of East London's vibrant queer scene. Loud and proud on Kingsland Road, it's still a liberated, hedonistic and decadent nightlife spot, with some of the most legendary parties in the city. No matter what you're into, you'll find it at Superstore. Want Bollywood? They've got you covered. What about classic pop or techno? Head down to the sweltering basement club and you might find both! Like Alice tumbling into Wonderland, you don't always know what you're in for, and that's part of the appeal. Open seven days a week, during the daytime the space invites people to hangout and use it as a place to work (no hidden desk charges,

either). Incredibly good-value food is served in the evenings and on weekends, when you can pop down for one of the iconic Drag Brunches (brunch but with drag queens!) Superstore also acts as an exhibition space, celebrating the work of LGBTQ+ artists and creators, and giving fledgling drag performers and DJs the chance to develop their craft. They host regular charity events and fundraisers for queer organisations.

The people put the *Super* in Dalston Superstore. Sure, it might be the coolest queer bar in London, but the regulars, performers, DJs, bar staff and bouncers all resist pretension. Their communal energy enters you the moment you step through the door, infusing every interaction you have, be it with your friends, strangers or potential lovers. You'll be BFFs with someone for the night, only to forget their name the next morning; or you'll take someone home thinking it's a one-night stand and end up happily married. Superstore is more than just be a 2,000 square foot bar in Dalston. It's a live, beating organism that feeds, protects and nurtures London's LGBTQ+ community.

THE KARAOKE HOLE
95 Kingsland High St, Dalston, E8 2PB
thekaraokehole.com
Nearest Tube: Dalston Kingsland Overground

From the creative minds behind Dalston Superstore, the Karaoke Hole is one of London's more unique spaces. Described as an 'LGBTQ+ powered venue' (meaning zero tolerance on homophobia, transphobia or harassment), the K-Hole, as it's lovingly referred to, is a chaotic karaoke bar with a difference. Instead of private booths, singers get on stage and sing their favourite songs in front of a live audience – aka, the

With an exhibition space and an inclusive atmosphere, Dalston Superstore has everything you could want for an alternate night out on the town.

The Queen Adelaide is proof that small can be special.

other punters. A different drag performer hosts each night, singing songs, manning a smoke machine, telling jokes and generally encouraging drunk people to sing along to Celine Dion. The drinks aren't too pricey – handy if you're nervous about hitting the stage. Patrons are receptive to anyone who has the chutzpah to sing, even if that person is tuneless. Despite this, you do get some incredible singers, and might even see someone performing '…Baby One More Time' with the full choreography if you're lucky. Be warned: it does get disorganised, especially as the night goes on. But by then you'll be sharing a bottle of Prosecco with someone you've just met, planning a duet of '(I've Had) The Time Of My Life'...

THE GLORY
281 Kingsland Rd, Haggerston, E2 8AS
theglory.co
Nearest Tube: Haggerston Overground Station

Before LGBTQ+ visibility went semi-mainstream and attitudes towards queer people shifted positive, the humble gay bar offered a refuge for LGBTQ+ people. They weren't just drinking dens or hook-up spots, but community spaces providing support and information, as well as safe spaces to socialise. Over the last two decades the holistic nature of queer venues started to dissipate. But with the sharp decline of LGBTQ+ venues in the capital over the last decade and a rise of anti-LGBTQ+ rhetoric and hate crimes, queer venues are once again becoming hubs for the community. This is personified by the Glory, a pub opened in 2014 by iconic London drag performers Jonny Woo and John Sizzle. On the surface, it's just another gay boozer – and a good one, too. There's ample seating, including sofas, a nice selection of beers and cocktails, and an outside smoking area. The bar staff

are convivial and the prices aren't absurd. On the weekends, the basement fills with queers getting their groove on – not that things are sedate upstairs. The main bar is always rammed, perfect if you don't mind squishing and sweating with a bunch of queer folx.

The Glory is far more than a pub. Since opening in late 2014, it has become one of London's premiere queer performance spaces. Woo and Sizzle often foster new talent. Many a drag king or queen, cabaret star and thespian has made their debut on the Glory's charming, if battered, stage. The annual Man Up! drag king contest and LIPSYNC1000 have become highlights of the queer social calendar. Beyond performance, Glory has hosted HIV/AIDS awareness events, events about queer history and talks centred on LGBTQ+ activism. For anyone ostracised by London's gay scene, the Glory offers a place all queers can call home.

THE OLD SHIP
17 Barnes St, Limehouse, E14 7NW
oldship.net
Nearest Tube: Limehouse Overground/DLR

The Docklands have always been a queer playground. In the 20th century, The Prospect of Whitby in Wapping was known to draw sailors and labourers who fancied themselves a feller, while the Shadwell Park Stairs in the Rotherhithe Tunnel had a reputation as a '30s cruising spot. That's not to mention the countless Molly houses, which in the 17th and 18th centuries drew all sorts of men who performed unspeakable deeds (see page 90). It shouldn't be surprising that tucked away on a corner just up from Limehouse station is an unassuming LGBTQ+ friendly pub that dates back to 1820. Managed by John Fell, who previously ran the now shuttered Booty's Riverside Bar, the pub is a proper East End boozer. Its charming frontage is like something ripped from a soap opera, but inside things get a little more subversive. Rainbows and kitschy knick-knacks accompany the traditional wood panelling. *Out* magazine once described it as 'a John Waters film set in Middle-earth'. Instead of the footie, the Old Ship hosts weekly cabaret and drag shows, drawing some of the city's best queens – including regular dame Saucy Sophie and Maisie Trollette, who at age 86 is the UK's oldest working drag performer. With two gay football teams and a ladies' dance troupe; along with regular fundraising events for the LGBTQ+ homeless charity, akt; the Old Ship keeps the Docklands' queer legacy alive.

THE QUEEN ADELAIDE
483 Hackney Rd, E2 9ED
thequeenadelaide.com
Nearest Tube: Bethnal Green

They say the best things come in small packages. That's certainly true for this beloved East London haunt. After the closure of iconic queer pub The George and Dragon, owners Liliana and Richard moved down the road to this lithe lot, filled with character. Ephemera adorns the red walls, including a cut out of Elvira, a sun with a smiley face, a poster of Divine and copious amounts of fairy lights. Towards the rear, a small bar offers your usual fare, on top of diverse alcy-free bevs for any non-drinkers. On the weekends, continue back past the loos (which leave something to be desired) and descend the stairs to enter The Queen Adelaide's labyrinthine basement club. One room is filled with antique furniture; another with seats. The walls are mirrored, and in the final room, sweaty bodies brush on the dancefloor. The Queen Adelaide has no formal event structure: one Saturday night might be queer

country themed, while the following week could be Britney vs. Christina. That's the ramshackle and, most importantly, inclusive nature of the Adelaide. This venue is capital 'Q' Queer, welcoming people of all sexualities, gender identities and presentations. The door staff hold this in mind, and any homophobic or transphobic nonsense is swiftly dealt with.

THE WHITE SWAN
556 Commercial Rd, Limehouse, E14 7JD
bjowhiteswan.com
Nearest Tube: Limehouse Overground/DLR

Something of an East End institution, the White Swan (previously BJ's White Swan) stood long before Shoreditch and Dalston blossomed into a queer playground. The pub was fairly seedy, with soft-core videos playing on screens. Yet it always drew crowds, and tended toward riotous on the weekends. Frequented by Sir Ian McKellen, this was where (allegedly) comedian Michael Barrymore came out. In 2014, however, the White Swan received a facelift that would leave Cher jealous. The pub was completely refitted, restructured and even extended with the addition of the neon-lit Funky Basement Club. Following its comeback, the White Swan began hosting cabaret, karaoke and drag shows, as well as club nights playing a mixture of pop, house and commercial dance on the weekends. Notably, it was home to anarchic queer party Cybil's House, an inclusive celebration of LGBTQ+ weirdness featuring dancing, performances and general madness. Open until 2am during the week, and even later on weekends, its raucous reputation remains, and unlike accusations levied at other queer East London venues, there's no pretension. As a bonus, if you cop off with someone, you can head next door to Sailors Sauna for a bit of fun.

Queer art can be found across the city, if you know where to look, such as outside The Glory on Kingsland Road.

JONNY WOO

Born Jonathan Wooster in Camberwell in 1972, Jonny Woo is the backbone of London's queer alternative drag, cabaret and theatre scene, which sprouted from East London in the 2000s. His work as a writer, actor and drag artist has seen him perform everywhere from the Royal Opera House to a field at the Glastonbury Festival. Jonny went to university in Birmingham before moving back to London to study at the London Contemporary Dance School in 1995. During this time he moved to Shoreditch and, needing money to pay for dance classes, found a job at a comedy café. After the owner paid for him to go to New York, Jonny relocated in 1999. Working under-the-counter and continuing to dance, he started to experiment with drag against the backdrop of the Big Apple's alternative arts scene, doing his first performance as a drag queen at The Slipper Room in the early '00s.

Not wanting to become an American, he moved back to London after three years in New York, taking over the flat of legendary drag performer and actor Lavinia Co-op in Hackney. Almost immediately, Jonny began hosting parties at the George and Dragon in East London. When restaurant-cum-queer venue Bistrotheque opened in 2004, he became something of a fixture, hosting drag lip-syncing competitions and, in his words, performing a different show each week for two months. It was around this period that he founded cult night Gay Bingo, which ran on-and-off for 10 years. Johnny took Gay Bingo everywhere, from the ICA to the Hackney Empire.

However, Jonny's lifestyle caught up with him. Feeling directionless, he made the decision to sober up in 2014. That same year, along with his partner at the time – fellow drag performer John Sizzle – he opened The Glory in East London, which has since become a cornerstone of London's queer scene. In addition to opening his own venue, Jonny has put on his Un-Royal Variety show at the Hackney Empire, which featured a smattering of some of the brightest and best cabaret, drag and nu-variety performers, and launched 'A Night at the Musicals' with collaborator Le Gateau Chocolat. Along with Sizzle, he has also been involved with the Riverstage, the National Theatre's outdoor festival of arts and entertainment. He staged 'Jonny Woo's All-Star Brexit Cabaret' with the Olivier Award-winning composer of Jerry Springer the Opera, Richard Thomas, in 2018. A regular feature at fringe festivals, both in the UK and abroad, Jonny is currently working on a play. Expect much more from him in the years ahead.

THE JOINERS ARMS AND
A HISTORY OF GAY NIGHTLIFE
IN EAST LONDON

There have been queer venues in London's East End for decades, operating both in and out of the shadows. But unlike Soho, the history of these spaces isn't well preserved; partly because, historically, East London hasn't been the most affluent or well-off area of the city, and partly because, like so much of queer history, little was documented due to fear of persecution. Of course, the East End had its fair share of Molly houses (gay brothels) and cruising spots, and according to Matt Houlbrook's book *Queer London: Perils and Pleasures in the Sexual Metropolis, 1918-1957* (University of Chicago Press, 2006), the sheer amount of men living in the lodging houses in the docklands meant homosexual relations were almost an inevitability.

In terms of pubs and clubs, though, the East End's history is murky. Still, there are definite examples dotted throughout the 20th century. The Railway Tavern pub in Limehouse, known locally as Charlie Brown's (after the landlord) drew in a queer crowd, operating from around 1840 to 1990. Likewise, there are reports of drag acts performing at the Royal Oak on Columbia Road between the 1940s and 1960s. Two performers, Lil and Maisie, were regulars. Had they been alive today, one of the pair, Lil, may well have identified as gender non-conforming or trans. Things become clearer in the '70s and '80s: pubs like the Arabian Arms (now Metropolis Strip Club) and the George IV in Limehouse became known for their cabaret and drag shows, while the London Apprentice on Old Street was famously a gay pub from the '70s to the '90s. Indeed, the L.A. was where the Terrence Higgins Trust's first meeting was held, and the venue even boasted a basement club call The Toolbox, which drew a leather and 'macho' crowd.

The area really came out the closet in the '90s and the '00s. In 1997, the Joiners Arms opened on Hackney Road. According to its manager, the late David Pollard, the pub was the first gay venue to open under Tony Blair's just-elected Labour government. Grotty and rough around the edges, it wasn't anything to look at, and in that first year, photographer Pollard operated a darkroom on the pub's first floor. He later cleaned things up – albeit only slightly. In 2002, the George and Dragon popped up just down the road. Richard Battye and Liliana Sanguino transformed this traditional boozer into a queer, kitschy fantasy, decked out with antiques that belonged to Battye's late grandmother. The George and Dragon even had its own exhibition space. The White Cubicle toilet gallery in the ladies' loos, founded by Pablo Leon de la Barra in 2005, exhibited work by the likes of Wolfgang Tillmans, General Idea, SUPERM (Brian Kenny and Slava Mogutin) and Terence Koh.

Such creativity spread into the rest of East London's queer scene. In 2006, Richard Mortimer, the founder of fashion magazine *Ponystep*, began his über-trendy party Boombox at Hoxton Bar and Grill, drawing an eclectic mix of fashionistas, musicians and artists. Meanwhile, nights like Gutterslut and underground electronic rave TrailerTrash gave things a bit of edge. In 2007, Dan Beaumont, Charlie Porter and Dave Kendrick began Macho City, a Hi-NRG disco party at the Joiners Arms every Thursday, which by 2009 *Gay Times* magazine had dubbed the 'most exciting gay venue in the UK'. Soon, creatives like Alexander McQueen, Rufus Wainwright and Christopher Kane were dropping in to this grotty, anarchic and electric queer pub. As the *New York Times* put it: 'Soho and Vauxhall may be the heart of London's *Queer as Folk*-watching, muscle-boy scene. But Shoreditch — fuelled by the creative energy of the city's East End — has emerged as a grittier, fashion-forward and often outrageous hotbed of gay night life.'

The Nelson's Head on Horatio Street completed the trifecta of the Joiners and the George, what later became known as the 'Shoreditch Triangle'. Opened in 2007, the pub had an early license, which meant queer folks would drop in on Sunday morning to continue the party, be that from the Joiners, the George and Dragon or further afield. The early morning drop-ins soon became unmanageable, however, and the pub began opening at a respectable 10am – though Sunday nights remained popular.

Around this time, the LGBTQ+ scene spread up Kingsland Road and into Dalston. Vogue Fabrics, later renamed vFd, opened in 2007. In 2009, Beaumont and Matt Tucker and Dan Hope, who ran TrailerTrash, established Dalston Superstore, which soon became the most fashionable place in the area. In 2010, Wayne Shires, a feature on the underground queer scene since 1989, opened his own venue, East Bloc, just off Old Street roundabout.

Still, the forces of gentrification and redevelopment reared their heads. In 2014, after successfully battling the council to keep its late license, the Joiners Arms lost its war against property developers. The pub shut

its doors for the final time in January 2015. The Nelson's Head befell a similar fate after rent increases, as did the George and Dragon. Battye and Sanguino managed to relocate, moving further down Hackney Road to their new spot at the Queen Adelaide, while the team from the Nelson's Head set up shop south of the river in Kennington. The Joiners, however, wasn't so lucky. Nevertheless, a community group, Friends of the Joiners Arms, successfully convinced Tower Hamlets council to stipulate that any new development built in the space must include a pub run as an LGBTQ+ venue for at least 25 years.

These closures were offset by the arrival of the Glory, the queer cabaret pub from Jonny Woo and John Sizzle. Similarly, parties like Sink the Pink, Savage, Mariah & Friendz, Chapter 10, Knickerbocker and, most recently, Adonis, provide an alternative to the queer club, making room for LGBTQ+ people in traditionally heterosexual spaces or unusual venues. As for the return of the Joiners Arms? At the time of writing, the pub's original building sits empty on Hackney Road. Thankfully, no matter what developers turn the space into, the Joiners will return.

The Joiners Arms, awaiting resurrection.

CLUBS

THE BACKSTREET
Wentworth Mews, Mile End, E3 4SP
thebackstreet.com
Nearest Tube: Mile End

Opened in April 1985, the Backstreet is the UK's longest running, and now sadly last, dedicated leather, rubber and fetish club. The door policy is as strict as it was over 35 years ago: if you ain't in leather, rubber or fetish attire, you ain't getting in. The club hasn't been updated since the '80s either, with boots and whips still hanging from the ceiling. But the Backstreet is all about atmosphere: in the front you'll find a more casual but cruisy bar area, while at the back, partitions and secluded areas offer privacy for people copping off. There's also an outdoor, partially heated smoking area, so you can enjoy a post-coital ciggie without having to walk the streets in whatever gear you've got on. Various slots across one night cater to different tastes: if you like to go nudie, you need Backstreet Unzipped; Fridays are for fetishes (think sports, human pups and skinheads); and there's even a monthly night for office wear. After 10pm, though, the Backstreet's signature strict dress policy comes into play, although visitors can borrow leather waistcoats and boots if they're without. If all that leaves you feeling intimidated, just know that the Backstreet has a reputation for being warm, friendly and sociable. Yes, the crowd skews a little older, but there aren't many clubs left in London where you'll come across gay men of all different ages. And the Backstreet looks set to stay, too: in 2019, Tower Hamlets council blocked plans to redevelop the site into a residential property, dubbing the Backstreet 'an important community asset'. They're not wrong.

BETHNAL GREEN WORKING MEN'S CLUB
42-44 Pollard Row, E2 6NB
workersplaytime.net
Nearest Tube: Bethnal Green

This venue has been a working men's club for over 133 years. In 2001, however, when faced with possible closure, the space opened its doors to non-members. It blossomed from there, becoming a hot spot for LGBTQ+ nightlife as well as gigs, burlesque and cabaret. Most notably, Sink the Pink called the club home in 2010, hosting their now legendary genderqueer parties in the upstairs room, while the more straight-laced club members nursed pints at the main bar downstairs.

Sink the Pink has moved on (although they regularly return for one-off parties). But that strange dichotomy between the club's sedate members and the flamboyant partygoers remains. The club's heritage stands strong; the place hasn't had a refit since the 1970s. The carpets are sticky and the decor threadbare, but that's part of its charm, and hasn't prevented BGWMC from hosting weird and wonderful club nights, artists, gigs and performances. Every Thursday, Friday or Saturday, you'll find some sort of madness in full swing, whether it's Mariah & Friendz, a monthly queer cabaret and dance party that's sort of (but not really) about Mariah Carey; karaoke, club nights celebrating pop queens, drag shows dedicated to Madonna and even queer country hoe-downs. Just don't be surprised if one of the O.G. East End working men's club members joins in on the fun.

THE BUNKER

217 City Rd, Hoxton, EC1V 1JN
ma1.co.uk
Nearest Tube: Old Street

Previously home to Wayne Shires's hedonistic queer club East Bloc, the Bunker was revamped by Alan Roberts (MA1) in 2019, giving this basement venue an X-rated overhaul. The dance floor has been transformed into a maze, sporting a cabin room, booths, glory holes, a sling and a darkroom, known as the 'Blackout Bunker'. Roberts, who previously hosted at the Backstreet and founded legendary naked night BUFF, set out to recreate the cruise bars of yore. The Bunker offers a variety of events. It's on the extreme side – think fisting nights, Club CP (a corporal punishment night) and mixed fetish parties. Still, there are less intense nights too, such as the London Jack Off Club (what it says on the tin) and Vicky's, a party for trans women, transvestites, couples and their admirers. The Bunker also offers a membership scheme, should you enjoy rabbiting around its warren of sleaze.

METROPOLIS

234 Cambridge Heath Rd, E2 9NN
metropolisclub.co.uk
Nearest Tube: Bethnal Green

It says a lot about the nature of London's ever mutating LGBTQ+ scene that one of the most popular new venues is a strip club. On Tuesdays, Wednesdays and Thursdays, Metropolis is a fully functioning gentleman's establishment, offering 'three floors of London's sexiest girls'. As soon as Friday hits though, the professional erotic dancers clock off, and Metropolis spends its weekend as a debauched dance den. The venue was popularised by Savage, a weekly club night organised by East Creative, the team behind Sink the Pink and queer festival The Mighty Hoopla. Originally a one-off party, Savage became the place you went *after* drinks, the sort of club night that still had a queue at 1am. Back then, Metropolis was fairly decrepit inside, and there was something fabulously subversive about letting loose in a strip club full of queers. Drag queens would work the poles, as would the punters. The top floor housed a room filled with sand and a hot tub, whereas the middle floor, clearly where gentlemen went to enjoy private dances, offered party goers some respite.

Savage ended in 2019. East Creative parted ways with Metropolis, although not before refitting the venue and installing a swish new sound system. The space was extended into the basement, making this a five-floored playground. On Saturdays, you'll now find Trash Palace, a mixed night playing House, R&B, hip hop and disco; or one-off DJ gigs. Fridays are reserved for Harpies, the UK's only LGBTQ+ inclusive strip club that centres trans and non-binary bodies (see page 62).

Both Savage and Harpies exemplify how LGBTQ+ people are able to claim heterosexual spaces by examining and exploring them outside the realm of gender binaries and heteronormativity. In the case of Metropolis, however, it's more of a *reclamation*. According to a call made in 1975 to the London Lesbian and Gay Switchboard (now just Switchboard) the venue was once a pub called The Arabian Arms that was 'mainly gay', with drag performances four times a week. It's a nice reminder of our continuity: that queer people have always been here and will always be here, too.

London's world-famous male leather bar, the Backstreet.

vFD

66 Stoke Newington Rd, Hackney Downs, N16 7XB
vfdalston.com
Nearest Tube: Dalston Kingsland Overground

vFd, previously known as Vogue Fabrics, may be the only club in the UK with Arts Council funding. It might also be the hottest club in London, quite literally – it gets so hot and sweaty that the walls are dripping by the end of the night. Opened in 2007 beneath owner and fashion designer Lyall Hakaraia's studio, the basement venue began as a space for queer artists and performers, before Dalston's nightlife boom. vFd soon became synonymous with the wildest parties in the area. The whole experience felt underground. Entering through the nondescript doorway and descending the stairs, you'd reach a small bar where drinks were served in small white plastic cups, the kind you find at a family BBQ, and a lawless dancefloor filled with the city's most fabulous queers. The bathrooms didn't have doors, separated from the outside world only by curtains.

Physically, little has changed (though vFd has put doors on the loos). Yet while the programming used to cater to the cis white gay crowd, the vFd of today is a bastion of alternative and inclusive events, hosting charity functions, experimental arts and theatre, festivals, poetry readings, live music, trans meet ups, femme and non-binary parties, nights for queer people of colour and even film screenings. Artists can exhibit their work in the Outsiders Gallery (i.e. the venue's front windows). Of course, if you want devilish disco and dancing, you'll find all that too – but like many other LGBTQ+ spaces in this area, vFd is more than just a club. It's a community.

THE WAYOUT CLUB

The Minories, 64-73 Minories, EC3N 1JL
thewayoutclub.com
Nearest Tube: Tower Hill

Founded in 1993 by Vicky Lee and the late Stuart Whitfield, the WayOut Club is London's oldest trans night. Hosted at the Minories pub in East London every Saturday, the night is open to people of all sexualities and gender identities. Unlike some other trans nights, WayOut focuses purely on socialising (no sex here), and maintains a friendly atmosphere. Lee is always open to conversations with new gals and guys. A strong community has developed over the years, and the night has diversified over the past 10 years to bring in a younger crowd. There aren't changing facilities, so visitors may want to rent a room nearby or travel in their outfits for the night. Guests can use the toilets, but be aware that they're shared with pub-goers before 11:30pm. Open until 3am, two rooms offer ample space for dancing and chatting. There's also a large, partially covered and heated outdoor seating area. The music is standard queer club fare (think house remixes of pop hits) and at 1am expect a performance from a drag artist or trans singer. Dedicated trans nights in London are few and far between, but almost everyone says that once you visit the WayOut Club, it feels like you've found a family.

This traditional strip club transforms into a queer wonderland every weekend.

vFd is packed with alternative events and arts.

CLUB NIGHTS

APHRODYKI
aphrodyki.com

Launched by founder Flo Perry in response to London's lacking lesbian scene, Aphrodyki is an Ancient Greece-themed night for queer womxn, lesbians, bisexual women, trans people and non-binary babes that celebrates the goddesses of pop and R&B. Men are allowed in, as are straight people, although there is a no-nonsense approach to harassment, homophobia, fat-phobia, racism and transphobia. After roaming various spots in East London, including one space in Dalston that didn't have nearly enough toilets, Aphrodyki can now be found at Miranda in the basement of the Ace Hotel, Shoreditch.

CHAPTER 10
chapter-ten.com

From the minds behind Dalston Superstore and the Karaoke Hole, Chapter 10, launched in 2014, is a queer rave. It plays music that, according to co-founder Dan Beaumont, 'has substance and means something to people'. Usually taking place once a month at Bloc in Hackney Wick, the night was born out of frustration with the city's gay scene and the lack of amazing DJs playing exclusively queer spaces. Chapter 10 is the sort of night that begs you to get lost in flashing lights and thumping beats. The main room is chocka with sweating bodies, all dancing their tits off. The eclectic, electric crowd is packed with people of all ages: hot men in mesh shirts join fashion-conscious non-binary folk and queer women in Adidas trainers and playsuits. However, expect a cis-het contingent who are drawn to the night because of its stellar line up of DJs and inclusive atmosphere. 'I think that if you're listening late at night to sweaty house and techno then there should be a lot of benders in the room,' Beaumont told *i-D* magazine. He's not wrong.

HARPIES
Metropolis, 234 Cambridge Heath Rd, E2 9NN
instagram.com/harpiesinthesky
Nearest Tube: Bethnal Green

Launched in July 2019, Harpies is the UK's first LGBTQ+ strip club. Founded by Lucia Blayke and hosted every Friday at Metropolis Gentlemen's Club (see page 57), the night focuses on trans and non-binary bodies, while representing the full spectrum of LGBTQ+ people. 'Our goal is to revolutionise the industry by changing the patriarchal structures of stripping and exotic dancing,' Blayke told *Dazed and Confused* magazine. 'We are taking back control over our fetishisation and putting money back into our own community. We aim to spread messages of love and acceptance for all LGBTQI+ people and solidarity with sex workers all over the world.'

Unlike traditional strip clubs, Harpies' dancers aren't charged a house fee, meaning they keep all the money they make while dancing. Guests are able to purchase 'tipping dollars', which dancers can exchange for cash tips, and even book private dances with people of all sexualities and genders. Of course, consent is essential, and anyone found overstepping will be ejected immediately. Visitors are vetted before entering, and there are strict rules about photography and filming to protect the identities of everyone involved. Harpies might be a celebration of the sex, bodies, eroticism and sensuality, yet it's also a safe space where people, especially trans people, are respected and looked after.

KNICKERBOCKER
facebook.com/knickerbockerparty

Founded in 2015, Knickerbocker is one of the best queer dance parties in East London. Usually housed in an unassuming, late-license art and performance space in Hackney Wick called The Yard, Knickerbocker is inclusive, open and friendly, with a zero-tolerance approach to harassment or abuse. Playing a mix of left-leaning pop from the likes of Robyn, Solange and Tho Knife, as well as harder electronic house music, the night also hosts performances and live art. Just don't be surprised by what you find on the stage – a noted example being someone inserting a tailed dildo, only to roam about wiggling it at people…

SHE WORLD
6 Leytonstone Rd, E15 1SE
she.world
Nearest Tube: Stratford

She World is a trans club in East London. Open every Saturday, they offer a safe and, should one wish, discreet space for the transgender community to get their groove on. Membership is required for entry, although it's free, and there's a dressing room with lockers should anyone want to change on-site. On the first floor you'll find more adult entertainment, including a movie lounge, darkroom and glory holes, while the basement contains a large play area. If you're lucky, you might spot the host, Sabrina, handing out After Eights. Fancy.

UNSKINNY BOP
unskinnybop.co.uk

Unskinny Bop began its life in 2002 as Ladyfest, a music and arts festival for feminist and women artists, as a way to celebrate the work of fat people in pop. It's since become a mainstay of London's queer scene. Having bounced around various spots in East London, it's found a home of sorts at The Star of Bethnal Green. The music has diversified, and now Unskinny Bop plays artists of all shapes, sizes and ages. Unskinny Bop is very popular with queer womxn, although it's open to people of all genders and sexualities. Always grounded in DIY zine culture (just check out one of their flyers), they even made their own zines for a while, which you could pick up across Soho in the 2000s. Kindness, acceptance and dancing are mandatory, and discrimination isn't tolerated. Whether you're fat, femme, butch, queer, trans, cis, non-binary or gay, you're welcome at Unskinny Bop.

WEST

BARS

TED'S PLACE
305 North End Rd, Hammersmith, W14 9NS
tedsplaceuk.co.uk
Nearest Tube: West Kensington

West London may no longer be the gay Mecca of the '70s, '80s and '90s, but that hasn't stopped the success of Ted's Place. This discreet basement bar opened in 1990. For 30 years, it provided a drinking spot for locals who can't face traipsing into Soho. The crowd tends a little older than your average night out down Old Compton Street, and on Fridays it's strictly men only, so expect cruising and darkroom fun. On Mondays, Thursdays and Sundays, however, Ted's hosts the city's longest running trans night, open to all trans people, cross-dressers, gender non-conforming folk, gay men and admirers. Known for its friendly atmosphere, visitors can either enjoy socialising or, if they're game, explore the 'play area'. Anything goes at Ted's Place.

WEST 5 BAR
Popes Ln, South Ealing Rd, W5 4NT
west5ealing.co.uk
Nearest Tube: South Ealing

West 5 used to be a New Zealand rock bar, until it pivoted queer in 1998. Since then, it's become one of London's most revered drag and cabaret bars, with local performers, drag acts and big-name Drag Race alumni all stamping their heels on the stage. Other regular nights include karaoke, live music and DJs.

There are a couple of rooms, so dancing queens will find ample space to shake their tail feathers, while the pool table may appeal for those after something more subdued. Regular drinks offers make this one of the cheapest LGBTQ+ spots in the capital (a vodka and mixer can sometimes cost only two quid!) and during the summer months the beer garden is crammed with hotties in their shortest shorts. West London doesn't have much on offer for queer people, but West 5 more than makes up for it.

EARL'S COURT'S GAY VILLAGE

From the 1970s to the 1990s, Earl's Court was London's gay ghetto. While LGBTQ+ venues dotted Soho, the East End and Vauxhall, Earl's Court's gay village wasn't just pubs, bars and discos: there were queer hotels, saunas, shops, cafés and restaurants. The area was popular with the city's LGBTQ+ population, mainly due to its (then) cheap housing. Large Victorian mansion blocks were transformed into bedsits, which also drew the city's transient populations, like those on temporary visas and backpackers.

The jewel in Earl's Court's gay crown was the Coleherne Arms on Old Brompton Road. Dating back to the 1880s, this pub had a reputation for drawing bohemian artist types – and in the 1930s you could supposedly find the odd drag artist performing after lunch. In 1955, the pub had become popular with gay men – as had the Boltons, another boozer just across the road. By the '70s, following the partial decriminalisation of homosexuality in 1967, the Coleherne had cemented itself as London's most famous gay pub.

The Coleherne had blacked-out windows to protect the identities of patrons, and the decor of the pub was decried as 'dreadful' by gay newspaper *Capital Gay*. Despite this, it was immeasurably popular, especially with the city's leather scene. The leather daddies, decked out in bikers' jackets, chaps and waistcoats, had their own side-door entrance, leading to the leather side of the bar. Anyone else used the main door. Never were the two groups to meet and mix.

Police were known to hassle customers in the area, with Tony Reeves, the former illustrator for *Gay News*, admitting that the police despised the pub. In 1976, *Gay News* reported that a fight between a customer and a policeman nearly turned riotous, leading to the formation of the Earl's Court Gay Alliance, a group to protect the local gay community from police harassment. Nearby Wharfedale Street and Brompton Cemetery were cruising areas for when the pub closed. Hopeful men would roam up and down into the early hours of the morning –

another thing that upset police, as well as prudish locals.

By the '80s, the Coleherne's reputation had only grown, with famous faces like Freddie Mercury, Ian McKellen, Kenny Everett and Derek Jarrman dropping by. Armistead Maupin even immortalised the pub in one of his 'Tales of the City' novels, *Babycakes*. People from all over the world came to visit the area, many staying at The Philbeach, a B&B with a cruisy reputation which only closed in 2008.

The Boltons had a seedier image, and was often frequented by sex workers and drug dealers. The Bromptons pub was popular with those intimidated by the leather and butch affectation of the Coleherne, although it provided no escape from the 'Clones': identikit gays who, not unlike many gay men in London's East End today, wore facial hair, check shirts and denim. Copacabana, which opened in the 1970s, was the country's first gay nightclub, and above that sat Harpoon Louis, a gay pub which held drag shows. In the early 1970s, the Masquerade was a disco operating from the basement of a laundrette. Likewise, next door to the Coleherne was the Catacombs, an unlicensed club where patrons on nights out often wound up drinking milk (the space has since been converted into a luxury home).

By the mid-to-late '90s, Earl's Court was falling out of favour with the gay community. Not only had property become unaffordable due to the area's proximity to Kensington, Chelsea and Fulham, but gay bars and clubs were opening in Soho, without the blacked-out windows symptomatic of the scene in the west of the city. There were attempts to inject a little more life into the district – the Coleherene was refitted in the '90s, as was Bromptons. But neither kept their clientele. The Coléherene is now a gastro-pub called The Pembrooke, while Bromptons has been demolished. By the 2000s, the Earl's Court gay scene had all but evaporated. Only one outpost of the gay outfitters, Clonezone, provides a physical memento of the area's significance to queer London history.

THE GATEWAYS CLUB

For decades the Gateways Club was a sanctuary for London's lesbian community. Opened in 1931, this unassuming member's club, located behind a green door at 239 King's Road on the corner of Bramerton Street in Chelsea, was popular with a bohemian crowd. When Ted Ware took it over after allegedly winning the venue during a poker game in 1943, the club became a place where gay, lesbian and Black people could meet in relative safety. Ware married the actress Gina Cerrato in 1953, and under their ownership the venue solidified its status as the best-known lesbian club in London. Soon, Gina and her right-hand woman, Smithy, an American who found her way to the UK through the US Air Force, began to run the club full time. In 1967, the club became women-only. It was known for being packed, with women dancing together in the small, sweaty space. In 1968, a year before the Stonewall Riots in New York, the club featured in the film *The Killing of Sister George*, with actual regulars featured as background actors dancing cheek-to-cheek – essentially outing themselves on screen. The club also featured in *The Microcosm*, the seminal 1966 lesbian novel by Maureen Duffy, who frequented the club.

In the 1970s and '80s, one thing separated the Gateways Club from other lesbian venues: Gina and Smithy's insistence that the club remain apolitical. They banned the Gay Liberation Front women from meeting there, and while feminist ideology and the Equal Pay Act of 1970 certainly had an impact, some found the discourse constricting, especially regarding femme and butch lesbian identities. Nevertheless, by the mid-1970s, butch-femme dynamics at the Gateways were beginning to wane. Similarly, the relationship between Smithy and Gina – whatever it may have been – also dissolved, though Smithy and her new girlfriend stayed on and worked at the club. Stiff competition from the multitude of discos and London's burgeoning LGBTQ+ scene forced the club to diversify, bringing in its own disco on Friday and Saturday nights.

Ted Ware died in 1979, an event that spelled the beginning of the end for the Gateways. Young, trendier lesbians preferred spots like the Bell in King's Cross, and while the Gateways underwent a refurb in the 1983, it couldn't battle against the competition – or rising rents in Chelsea, which by then had become a very affluent area. In 1985, the club lost its late license, and on 24 September of that year the Gateways closed its doors forever.

PORCHESTER HALL DRAG BALLS

Running from 1968 until the 1980s, the Porchester Hall Drag Balls were some of the first events to bring queer life out into the open – truly the highlight of the queer social calendar. Started by Jean Frederick, a trombone-playing Canadian drag queen, and fellow drag queen Ron Storme, just a year after the partial decriminalisation of homosexuality, the balls were so popular that people travelled to the event from across the UK. Resplendent queens swept up and down the Porchester Hall's dramatic marble staircase, while the building's main room was the perfect extravagant setting for the flamboyant costumes and themed outfits. Central to each night was the pageant competition, where performers would walk a makeshift catwalk to win a prize consisting of either cash (around £25, a significant amount in the day) or, as the time progressed, a trip abroad. Fredericks was even known to play the trombone, should the opportunity arise. The crowd didn't just consist of drag queens; all members of the queer community were welcome, and some guests may have identified as trans or non-binary, had such language been common at the time. After Frederick's death in the late '70s, the drag balls at Porchester continued, although Storme began hosting his own events at the Tudor Lodge in the East End. However, things went awry in 1986: Denis Gilling, a London theatre entrepreneur, hosted a number of BDSM events called 'Feather, Leather, Flesh and Whiplash', which ultimately led the governors of the Porchester Hall to ban the drag balls for good.

Home to some of the best drag balls of the late 20th century.

SOUTH

BARS

THE BRIDGE

8 Voltaire Rd, Clapham Town, SW4 6DQ

bridgewinebar.com

Nearest Tube: Clapham North/Clapham High Street Overground

While some LGBTQ+ venues have notions of grandeur, it would be a reach to call them sophisticated. The Bridge, however, is as close as it comes. Describing itself as a 'wine bar', it serves from a compact joint just off Clapham High Street. It's not cheap, but the winelist is decent, and you can find interesting cocktails as well as happy-hour deals. It's more relaxed than anything you'll find in Vauxhall, and certainly more chilled than the nearby Two Brewers. It would be the perfect spot for a quiet date, although any intimacy might get interpreted during the week by various events such as movie nights, a quiz, bear night and drag bingo. The music combines House and Top 40 hits, and the mainly-male crowd, while a smidge older than some spots, is still comprised of tight t-shirt wearing hotties and lushy young professionals. In the summer, people watching (aka cruising) from the benches outside is a must.

CMYK

105 - 109 The Broadway, Wimbledon, SW19 1QG

barcmyk.co.uk

Nearest Tube: South Wimbledon

Local queer venues are few and far between, and LGBTQ+ residents of Wimbledon are some of the lucky ones. Opened in 2019, Bar CMYK (standing for Cyan, Magenta, Yellow and Key, the four colours used in printing to create the entire rainbow) boast that they're the first LGBTQ+ bar in Wimbledon. They've done a fine job – the bar is decked out in style, with tasteful colours schemes, trendy yellow seating, neon lighting and lots of marble. They've even kept the original 1920s tiling in the downstairs club, which is very chic. The cocktail list is extensive, and decently priced, and there's a healthy winelist plus your usual beers and spirits. Expect heaps of cabaret and drag, as well as singing competitions and club nights that run until 4am. Wimbledon just got a little more fabulous.

THE COCK TAVERN

340 Kennington Rd, Oval, SE11 4LD

thecocktavernlondon.com

Nearest Tube: Oval

For years, this pub in Kennington was known as South London Pacific, a rather tired tiki bar that brought out the best and worst of straight young professionals hunting for that weekend release. When the venue closed in 2017, it was taken over by Farika Holden and her partners Patrick Black and Leean James – the wranglers behind infamous queer East End joint the Nelson's Head, who were looking for a new home after rising rent prices forced them to shut up shop. Giving the place a refurb, they reinstated the pub's original name, the Cock Tavern, as well as its queer heritage (the venue was a gay bar many moons prior). The new interiors are dark and seductive: all black paint, white panelling and red accents, with paintings covering the walls and ceiling. The large, L-shaped wooden bar serves up cocktails, craft beers and an impressive winelist. If you head to the back of the pub, you'll find remnants of the establishment's tiki past, with bamboo decal and carved, decorative masks haunting the makeshift dance floor. The crowd consists mostly of gay men during the week, but things do diversify on the weekends. It definitely draws a more alternative crowd than other South London haunts, appealing to those put off by the late night antics of the Eagle, who are after something less intense than the Royal Vauxhall Tavern (although some start their night at the Cock and move on to those places, clasping gins in tins from a nearby off license). On Wednesdays, the legendary jukebox is free – a Nelson's staple that houses a whole host of gay classics – and on Sunday the weekly pub quiz often gets rowdy, with drag queens and nudity par for the course.

THE GEORGE AND DRAGON
2 Blackheath Hill, Greenwich, SE10 8DE
georgedragon.com
Nearest Tube: Deptford Bridge Overground/DLR

This cabaret bar might share a name with the now closed but legendary East London boozer the George and Dragon, but that is where their similarities end. This George and Dragon is a proper local boozer, traditionally decorated and not fussed with trendy affectations. There is a very healthy drag and cabaret schedule, but don't expect the subversive stuff you encounter across the Thames. The queens here are old-school – but still camp, acerbic and filthy. On Fridays and Saturdays it's best to arrive after 10pm. It can be disconcertingly quiet before then, although it never fills up like the bars in Soho. To some that

might be off-putting, but the George's provincial atmosphere is one of its best attributes. Unfussy and affable, you're unlikely to encounter any stuffiness from the staff – or your fellow punters, who are usually friendly and up for as much fun as you are. Plus, the drinks offers are a steal (a pint for three quid!), and it's open until 2am most nights and 4am on weekends. This might not be the shiniest toy in London's queer playbox, but there's nothing wrong with a well-loved, if weathered favourite. This old queen George still stands for a reason.

THE ROYAL VAUXHALL TAVERN
372 Kennington Ln, Vauxhall, SE11 5HY
vauxhalltavern.com
Nearest Tube: Vauxhall

With its long history, the Royal Vauxhall might just be the most beloved LGBTQ+ venue in London. During the week you'll find experimental theatre, cabaret and drag performances, though the RVT remains a spot where you can go and enjoy a quiet pint when there's not an old queen stomping the stage. Weekends are reserved for club nights, including popular events like alternative queer night Duckie, '90s and '00s pop at Push The Button, '80s fun at Frankie Goes To Vauxhall, bear night Beefmince and more. The weekly Sunday Social, an afternoon of cabaret and drag followed by an evening of dancing, is a highlight. Whatever catches your fancy, it's worth buying tickets in advance, as they often sell out.

A typical Friday night at the RVT sees the venue at capacity. The seating (put out for shows during the week) is removed, and hundreds of sweaty queers and allies pack in to dance to Carly Rae Jepsen.

There's an outside smoking area, which is worth taking advantage of to cool down, although after a certain time no drinks are allowed outside. The bar, which lines the right-hand wall, is always at the centre of a crowd – but the staff are friendly, understanding and up for a laugh, as long as the people they're serving are patient. The only problem is that you're likely to turn around, four pints in plastic cups grasped precariously between your hands, only to knock into a handsome fella or non-binary beauty and spill beer down your front. If you don't mind getting sweaty and covered in booze, there's no place in London quite like it.

Stepping through the doors feels like you've come home, and the atmosphere is so unpretentious, accepting and kind that even if you lose your friends (an impressive feat, as the place isn't huge), you'll be set for the night with whomever you end up dancing with. Community is a word that often gets thrown around when discussing LGBTQ+ venues, but the RVT really does exude community spirit. You might only be a part of that community for one night, but when you're inside the venue's red walls, between podiums, the cramped stage, the old-fashioned bar, and hundreds of LGBTQ+ folk having the time of their lives, it's like being part of the most fabulous family.

THE TWO BREWERS
114 Clapham High St, Clapham Town, SW4 7UJ
the2brewers.com/london
Nearest Tube: Clapham Common

Opened in 1981, the Two Brewers is such an institution that even the staunchest North Londoners will cross the Thames for a visit. Cabaret is the Brewers's calling card, and it regularly hosts some of the city's most fabulous kings and queens, including

RuPaul's Drag Race alumni and legendary Aussie performer Pam Ann (aka Caroline Reid), comedians and musical guests (former Sugababes star Mutya Buena has been known to get on the mic). While it operates as a pub during the week (albeit one with a late license) the back opens up on the weekends, revealing a club that draws a mixed crowd of gays, gals and pals who are looking to slut drop to The Saturdays. It's particularly good if you're on the pull, with many men looking for a midnight snack. It was given a lick of paint in 2018, which was long overdue, although modernisation is offset by the sparkling gold wall behind the stage. The venue's general air of camp is – like the sticky floors – impossible to get rid of.

Capable of drawing crowds from across the river, the Two Brewers is the place to cruise.

Bearing a long LGBTQ+ legacy, it isn't a stretch to call the RVT London's most beloved queer venue.

THE RVT: LONG MAY SHE REIGN

Built as a public house between 1860 and 1862 on the site of the old Vauxhall Pleasure Gardens, the Royal Vauxhall Tavern has always been closely aligned with the city's queer population. Back in the 18th century, the Pleasure Gardens hosted Masquerades that drew many cross dressers, including the infamous Princess Seraphina (known as such in and out of female drag). The gardens were also a favourite prowl of 'sexual deviants', with unlit 'dark walks' serving as an old-fashioned cruising ground – although both men and women got up close and personal.

After the Second World War, gay servicemen began frequenting the RVT, and by the 1950s drag performances, which took place on the bar owing to the venue's lack of a stage, had become a part of the pub's DNA. At that time, homosexuality was illegal. Records are scant as a result, but we do know that the pub was split into three sections by partition walls, each one had its own entrance, and a large bar served them all. While one of these sections served heterosexual drinkers, another was used primarily by queer clientele. 'The biggest part was the gay part,' said legendary drag performer and activist Bette Bourne, who visited the pub in the '50s, 'because it was packed and that was the part that made the money.'

After the partial decriminalisation of homosexuality with the Sexual Offences Act of 1967, the RVT's LGBTQ+ and heterosexual visitors began to mix, and by the '60s and '70s the pub became one of London's premiere destinations for alternative entertainment, cabaret and drag. A heterosexual couple called Pat and Breda McConnon, were the landlords from 1979 to 1993. They desegregated the space, ripping out the long, curved bar, which had been installed in the late 1800s by architect R.A. Lewcock, to fit a stage and more seating.

By the 1980s, the RVT, while still a mixed venue, had become a pivotal space on London's burgeoning gay scene. 'I think [gay people] come here and are able to let themselves go a bit more,' Breda McConnon told *Gay Life*, a documentary series broadcast by London Weekend Television in 1980. 'They can see it on the stage, and I think that drag is [them] doing their own thing, really.'

'It had a much more colourful feel than other venues.' So Chris Smith, Baron Smith of Finsbury and the first MP to come out as gay, told Ben Walters, who did a PhD on the Royal Vauxhall Tavern club night, Duckie. 'Most of the places I visited were either serious drinking or serious dancing but the Vauxhall was more of a burlesque place. It had more colour and life.'

If the RVT was a sanctuary for queer people in the late '70s and early '80s, by the mid '80s that refuge had cracks. The AIDS crisis had decimated London's gay community, and anti-LGBTQ+ attitudes were on the rise. The RVT was raided by police throughout the late '80s. During one raid in 1986, landlady Breda McConnon and three members of staff were arrested for selling poppers, which weren't technically illegal.

In 1987, while Lily Savage (the drag alter-ego for television personality Paul O'Grady, for those not in-the-know) was performing, 34 police officers, all wearing rubber gloves, descended on the RVT. The home office claimed that the gloves were worn 'to protect officers from the risk of infection by Hepatitis B or AIDS as a result of accidental injury from any drugs paraphernalia', although it was clear they stood for something far more sinister: a visual reminder of society's aversion to homosexuality and queer people.

'The door was burst in, this copper came in, and of course, I thought he was a stripper,' O'Grady recalled in an

interview with filmmaker Tim Brunsden. 'As you would...
He said, "Come on you, out!" I said, "Who the fucking hell
are you talking to?" I'm there dressed in a corset and boots.
Then it suddenly clicked: I looked over his shoulder and the
pub was full of police... It wasn't a good time to be gay.'

Nevertheless, the RVT stood resilient, regularly hosting
benefits and fundraisers for funerals and HIV/AIDS
awareness. 'The Vauxhall raised thousands,' O'Grady
recalled. 'We used to buy things like mattresses for
them in the hospitals, pillows, sheepskin rugs... We
were the soldiers. We were the Vera Lynns of south
London! Meanwhile, we had the same problems they
[the audience] did, and they knew that. Bloody great
camaraderie. There was a very strong community spirit.'

During this time, legend has it that even royalty made
their way to the RVT. According to actress Cleo Rocos,
on one night in 1988, Queen frontman Freddie Mercury,
comedian Kenny Everett, herself and Princess Diana
all made their way to the pub. Diana was said to be 'in
full mischief mode', and to avoid being photographed
Mercury dressed her as a boy in a camouflage jacket,
black leather cap and sunglasses. 'She did look like a
beautiful young man,' Rocos wrote in her book, *The
Power of Positive Drinking*.

In the 1990s and early 2000s, Vauxhall blossomed into
a gay village, with clubs like The Hoist, Fire and Crash.
In 1995, visionary performance collective Duckie began
hosting regular cabaret shows and club nights at the Royal
Vauxhall Tavern as an alternative to the homogenised
LGBTQ+ scene in London, which focused on gym-
buff cisgender males. Duckie was a hit, rowdy with
disenfranchised queers and weirdos who kept coming
back to experience the non-conventional performances
that made the night popular. In fact, Duckie's success

was one reason why 1998 plans from Lambeth Council
to knock down the RVT and build a supermarket were
thrown out.

Further nights, like the cheesy, pop-loving Push The
Button and Bar Wotever, a meet up for queer performers
and creatives that advocates for trans and non-binary
communities, only cemented the pub's position as
London's premiere alternative queer venue. Nowadays, the
RVT is popular with LGBTQ+ people from all walks of life.

The RVT's celebrated status hasn't kept it safe from
threats. In 2014, it was revealed that the venue had been
sold to property developers, who refused to meet with
the locals about their wish to redevelop the space. A
month after the news broke, a group of RVT veterans,
regulars and performers formed. Known as RVT Future,
the group successfully secured an Asset of Community
Value status for the pub, which prevented any immediate
development plans and allowed them to put a bid on the
pub, should it be sold. Ben Walters, a member of RVT
Future, submitted a 15,000-word application making the
case for the RVT to become a listed building. After some
wobbles, and a further 15,000-word supplementary
submission featuring letters and stories from famous
faces and politicians, Historic England granted a Grade II
listing to the building, making it the first building in Britain
to be listed for its significant LGBTQ+ history. Years of
back and forth between Lambeth Council, RVT Future
and property developer Immovate ensued, but in 2018
the CEO/Managing Director of the Royal Vauxhall Tavern,
James Lindsay, secured a 20-year lease.

Of course, London's LGBTQ+ scene is in constant
flux, existing on a precipice. But hopefully 20 years will
become 50, and 50 will become 100. The RVT is true
LGBTQ+ royalty, after all. Long may she reign.

CLUB NIGHTS

C.Y.O.A.
facebook.com/cyoa.ldn

Choose Yr Own Adventure (C.Y.O.A) is a sober LGBTQ+ dance party. Designed for queer folk who want a night on the town without intoxication, C.Y.O.A. is open to queer people of all sexualities, genders (or lack thereof), backgrounds, ages and body types. Playing a mix of Robyn, Rihanna and riot grrrl, C.Y.O.A. proves you can have a blast without the booze.

DUCKIE
duckie.co.uk

Ever since London's queer scene came out of the closet, it's been dogged by accusations of homogeny. And, depending on who you ask, rightly so. Pubs and clubs have always favoured cisgender gay men, and from the clones of the '70s and '80s to the birth of the gym-bunny Muscled Mary in the '90s and '00s, anyone who doesn't conform, be it because of their gender, body, sexuality or taste, can feel like an outcast. In the late '90s, London's LGBTQ+ scene was very driven by men, the nights either playing new-fangled techno and house music or pop hits. Disenfranchised queers didn't have many options available. In 1995, inspired by the arrival of indie club night Popstarz, a group of six friends – Amy Lamé, Simon Casson (aka Simon Strange), DJs Kim Phaggs and Chelsea Kelsey (aka the London Readers Wifes) and Jay Cloth and Father Cloth (known now as the Door Whores) – put together Duckie, an inclusive LGBTQ+ night where performance, drag, art and anti-theatre could merge with drinking and dancing to alternative pop music.

Now, 25 years later, Duckie is still, as Lamé described it, a 'club of outcasts'. Operating every Saturday night, it's a melting pot of ideas, personalities and cultures, soundtracked to an eclectic mix of Britney, Blur and Bowie. The weekly stage show could see you witness an epic lip sync, or someone inserting an upright vacuum cleaner handle up their bottom – you never know what you'll get.

Since its inception, Duckie has diversified its offerings, be it organising tribute nights to Kate Bush at the ICA, experimental performance and theatre at the Barbican or hosting events at the Tate. Their work includes community outreach, with projects engaging older LGBTQ+ people and homeless people, as well as offering schemes for young performers, including the Duckie Homosexualist Summer School.

Each year, Duckie hosts Gay Shame on the date of London Pride, 'an annual festival of homosexual misery' that most recently took place at the Royal Vauxhall Tavern and extended into the arches. It acts as an alternative to the commercialised Pride events. Not miserable in the slightest, it's a complete and utter blow out.

Duckie is grounded, however, by their weekly party at the RVT, which shows no signs of stopping. Every Saturday it's still jampacked with queer people and their allies looking to let loose and explore the wackier side of London nightlife. Always irreverent, utterly incomparable and totally iconic: Vive la Duckie!

HORSE MEAT DISCO
facebook.com/horsemeatdisco

Dubbed 'the queer party for everyone', Horse Meat Disco has been a staple on London's LGBTQ+ scene since 2004. Born out of a basement in Soho, the night pays homage to the New York clubs of the '70s and '80s. Co-founded by James Hillard and Jim Stanton, with additional resident DJs Severino and Luke Howards, HMD takes place every Sunday at the Eagle, where you'll find these four playing a kaleidoscopic selection of Italo disco, house, dance music oddities, punk funk and, of course, disco in all its iterations. The DJs also tour the festival circuit, taking over various clubs throughout the capital, as well as venues around the world. The crowd is always diverse: club kids, fashionistas, ladies, bears and drag queens all make their way south on a Sunday to mingle and make out. Horse Meat Disco's bank holiday parties are particularly infamous, with London's queers and hetero disco-lovers celebrating their extra day of freedom under the sparkling lights of the disco ball.

PUSH THE BUTTON
pushthebutton.org.uk /www.facebook.com/ PTButton

Push The Button has a strict remit: if a song was recorded outside of the years between 1990 and 2020, it's not getting played. This monthly party at the Royal Vauxhall Tavern is a pop lover's fantasy, playing everything from STEPS to Selena Gomez. If it was a hit over the last 30 years, it'll likely get a spin. It almost always sells out each month, and is crammed with friendly LGBTQ+ people and pop music fans who aren't afraid to go disco dancing with the lights down low. The organisers deck the place out with lollipops and sweeties (in summer months you might get an ice lolly), and there's always a group sing-a-long to a power-ballad, as well as a drag performance in the early hours of the morning. A close community of

people come to almost every PTB, so if you become a regular, you'll see the same faces and, undoubtedly, be welcomed into the fold. Push The Button also organise a number of special events, including the now legendary Push The Button: Spice Up Yer Life, a chaotic and brilliant night that sees Spice Girls fans board the Spice Bus (not the actual bus from the movie *Spice World*, but an old double decker) and stop off at various iconic landmarks from the film until they arrive, inebriated and filled with Girl Power, at the RVT to spend the rest of the night. At Push The Button there's no such thing as a guilty pleasure, and nothing is deemed cheesy. This is a night for those passionate about pure, unadulterated pop.

ROMA TRANS CLUB
facebook.com/romapartylondon

This monthly party is open to transgender people, transvestites, crossdressers, couples and single admirers. The club night recently moved to the Fire complex in Vauxhall, where guests can dance the night away or slope off to find somewhere more intimate.

BBZ

Meet BBZ: a queer Black art and nightlife collective from South East London. Founded in April 2016 by Tia 'Sippin' T' Simon-Campbell and Naeem Davis, BBZ began as a club night and exhibition space for queer Black and brown womxn, trans and non-binary people to meet and for queer artists of colour to display their work. The night was an instant success, and BBZ's vision to create spaces specifically for queer, trans and non-binary people of colour was born. As it grew in popularity, more and more people wanted to support the group, creating a truly collective atmosphere. As Tia has said, if people have the time and space to contribute regularly, BBZ will try to make any collaboration work.

The collective's relationship with *gal-dem* magazine founder, Liv Little, led to BBZ being invited to DJ and exhibit at the V&A. In 2017, BBZ took over the Tate Exchange for a week in a project that saw them explore Blackness and queerness in different ways, be it through initialisations, films, club nights, workshops, letter writing or the hosting of a co-working space. Out of that collaboration sprung the BBZ Black Book (BBZ BLK BK), a digital directory of queer Black and brown creatives and artists. The following year, inspired by the Black Book project, BBZ organised their first Alternative Graduate Show at the Copeland Gallery. Open to any recent graduates with Black ancestry who identified as queer womxn, trans or non-binary, the show highlighted the work of 10 emerging artists. It also provided a holistic approach: offering artists insight into how exhibitions are put together, while hosting workshops on how to price one's work, write CVs and approach galleries. This led to another graduate show in 2019.

During this time, BBZ continued to host parties, collaborating with fellow collectives like Pxssy Palace and institutions like the Southbank Centre. In 2020, the collective wiped their social media accounts clean. They announced that, following a number of commercial partnerships and brand collaborations, 2020 would be 'all about returning to our roots of prioritising, celebrating and platforming the folx that got us here in the first place.' It's time to get reacquainted with BBZ.

Photograph by Tia Simon-Campbell

NO FIXED ABODE

CLUB NIGHTS AND COLLECTIVES

THE BATTY MAMA
facebook.com/TheBattyMama

Founded by queer artists and programmers Ama Josephine Budge, Hakeem Kazeem and Lasana Shabaz, the Batty Mama is a night for QTIBPOC (queer, trans, intersex, Black people & people of colour) by QTIBPOC. Playing a mix of '90s R&B, hip hop, garage, afrobeats basement, funky house and Detroit techno, the nights always include some kind of surprise performance. On hand are the Batty Buddies, too, who offer support, reassurance, hugs, or dance-offs (consent required, naturally).

BRÜT
instagram.com/brutlondon

This roaming men-only night is for bears, blokes, hunks and their admirers. It's sweaty, cruisy and goes hard until the early hours of the morning.

BUTCH, PLEASE!
butchplease.co.uk

There aren't many nights in London that centre and celebrate female masculinity, which is why Butch, Please! was born. Started in 2015 by self-described 'butch dyke', singer-songwriter Tabs Benjamin, this trans and non-binary inclusive night usually finds its home at the Royal Vauxhall Tavern or The Glory. It's open to 'Butch Muthers and Baby Dykes alike', as well as people of all genders and sexualities. There are usually live performances from drag kings and other artists, skill shares and, occasionally, orgasm competitions. The nights often have a theme, which have previously included leather and denim nights, Rockabilly and the iconic Night of a 1000 K.D. Langs, which was endorsed by the 'Constant Craving' singer herself. The music is eclectic and the crowd electric, and everyone is there to celebrate butchness.

THE CHATEAU
thechateau.org.uk

For nearly two years, the Chateau was the most exciting new queer venue in London. Tucked away in a cosy basement in Camberwell, this DIY LGBTQ+ club was dubbed a 'pop up bar and cultural space' run by queers, for queers. Open on the weekends, they held an vibrant mix of club nights, fundraisers, events and performances, with an equally diverse crowd of chic gender non-conforming patrons. Its unique decor – stained glass windows and wooden banquettes – gave the place a sanctified aura, and a night twirling on the dance floor to some insane pop music was truly a religious experience. In 2020, however, the Chateau announced that its time in Camberwell had come to an end. But pop ups do move on, and as they said in their statement: 'The Chateau is an entity without walls and WE WILL CONTINUE.' Be sure to be there when it does.

CLUB KALI
clubkali.com

Club Kali is the longest running Asian music night for LGBTQ+ people in the UK – not to mention the largest in the world. Founded in 1995 by Rita and DJ Ritu, two South Asian women, the night plays a mix of bhangra, Bollywood, Arabic, house, R&B, dance classics and contemporary pop hits. In the '90s, it provided queer Desi people with a safe space that celebrated a multitude of different South Asian cultures and heritages, a role it stills serves today. Trans people, drag performers and chutney queens – a take on drag influenced by South Asian culture – all found a home at Club Kali. The night now draws a crowd of people from many different backgrounds, with queer folx from across the world making their way to their monthly parties. Club Kali also host events at the ICA, the V&A and the BFI.

CHAIN REACTION

Chain Reaction was the UK's first lesbian fetish night, running in the 1980s. Founded by the Rebel Dykes, a group of political and sexually liberated feminist lesbians living in London in the '80s, the night began its life in a King's Cross club before moving to the Market Tavern in Vauxhall. Known for being explicit, with live sex shows, S&M and stripping, the night met resistance from certain members of the LGBTQ+ community – especially a group who called themselves the Political Lesbians. These were conservative, anti-men campaigners who, according to activist, filmmaker and artist Siobhan Fahey, rejected anything that resembled heterosexuality, including 'butch and femme, fantasies that involved anything masculine, power play' and phallic adult toys. As documented in the film *Rebel Dykes*, during the second Chain Reaction event the 'political lesbians' raided the club night (although they were chased off, which only increased Chain Reaction's popularity). 'I think people just finally wanted to be sexual in a world where being a lesbian had become extraordinarily celibate, feminist and right on,' Fahey told *Vice*. 'People wanted to put a finger up to that and create something more outrageous.'

HUNGAMA
facebook.com/hungamaldn

Ryan Lanji started Hungama to explore the diasporic experiences of queer South Asians. He melded the Western music that he had grown up loving – hip hop, R&B – with the Bollywood sounds that represented his cultural heritage. The name *hungama* comes from an Urdu word meaning 'disorder' or 'chaos' – fitting, because when you're out at Hungama, anything is possible. The night, which takes place monthly at varying venues across London, is filled with the most fabulous LGBTQ+ folk, South Asian drag queens, queer men and women, trans people and non-binary folx and their allies all living out their fantasies on the dance floor. As Lanji has said, Hungama imagines 'what it could look like if Studio 54 was Indian'. For a long time, LGBTQ+ South Asian people have felt like they needed to choose between their culture and their sexuality or gender identity. At Hungama they no longer have to.

The Eagle, home to Horse Meat Disco, a queer party for all.

LET'S HAVE A KIKI
instagram.com/letshaveakikildn

Strike a pose at Let's Have A Kiki, a queer party serving up the voguing scene of '80s and '90s Harlem in modern day London. Hosted by dancer and DJ Jay Jay Revlon (of the House of Revlon), this community-focused club night is open to everyone, as long as you're prepared to be yourself, strut your stuff, turn it out and have a good time.

LICK
facebook.com/LICKeventsUK

LICK is London's only night run by womxn for womxn. Founded by Teddy Edwardes, the night has a strict no men policy – meaning *all* men, trans or cisgender. The night, open to womxn in all their forms and non-binary folx, plays a heady mixture of hip hop and R&B. LICK also hosts live events, with the likes of Ms Banks, Etta Bond and Lady Leshurr all performing. They've also put on womxn and non-binary people-only stripping events at For Your Eyes Only, a strip club on City Road, as well as at Metropolis. Lesbians, queer womxn, trans women and non-binary people are so often overlooked by London's queer scene. LICK shows they don't have to settle. Or, as Edwardes told *Time Out:* 'It's extremely important that we get more representation for trans, non-binary and queer people of colour; that's where LICK comes in.'

LITTLE GAY BROTHER
littlegaybrother.com

Little Gay Brother was formed at the now defunct festival Secret Garden Party in 2012 by Clayton Wright as a space for LGBTQ+ festival goers to feel safe and 'party without prejudice'. It was so popular they began hosting regular nights at Dalston Superstore, before expanding to bigger club venues, such as FOLD, Hangar, Omeara and even superclub Fabric. In that time, the club night has become much more than a party. Little Gay Brother is a collective that boasts over 100 creatives, from dancers, DJs, promoters, performers, drag artists, designers and more; made up of a mixture of gay, straight, queer, trans and gender non-conforming individuals. Their parties are spectacles, with dancing and drag performances, all soundtracked to a delicious and electric mix of house, techno and disco that has defined queer club culture for decades. Completely undefinable, Little Gay Brother has also hosted street parties, festival tents and dance recitals at the Royal Academy of Arts, and even has plans to host a weekender in Ibiza. Unapologetically queer, gloriously incisive and really quite fabulous, Little Gay Brother is an uninhibited and inclusive fixture of London's queer landscape where people can emphatically be themselves.

MISERY
instagram.com/miseryparty

Misery is a sober club night and party for queer, trans, intersex people of colour and their allies with a focus on mental health and neurodivergencies. Founded by Aisha Mirza, a writer, DJ and counsellor, Misery parties support and uplift QTIPOC in a space that is non-judgemental and safe. Along with workshops, vegan food and mental health resources, you'll find genderless nail bars, art, tactile play corners, performances and, of course, dancing. There's even a trained mental health professional in attendance, who can be accessed through their One To Hun service. They give party goers the chance to share how they're feeling or to get things off their chest (please be aware, however, that this isn't a crisis service). Sober spaces can be daunting, and if you're anxious or riding solo you can be buddied up with a 'misery mate'. Alongside their nightlife offerings, they organise other therapeutic events, including cooking classes, foraging and twerkshops. 'No one wants to be sad all the time,' Mirza wrote for *i-D*, 'but Misery is an invitation to come as you are, to talk and heal collectively, to be sad or quiet in public, to celebrate, and to give gratitude for those before us and around us who have not had that option.'

PXSSY PALACE
instagram.com/pxssypalace

Pxssy Palace is everything that's right about London's diversifying queer scene. The night was started by Glaswegian exports Nadine Artois and Skye Barr out of their Brick Lane flat after the pair became disenfranchised by London hip-hop clubs. Their house parties soon became legendary, with everyone begging for entry, and soon Artois and Barr expanded to proper venues while snapping up a talented group of producers, DJs, photographers, and creatives. The ethos of the night was what bound them all: to create a safe space for queer womxn, intersex, non-binary and trans people of colour and their allies to party. Pxssy Palace provides free taxi services for trans femmes of colour, which are funded by money collected on the door and 10% of the earnings from the night. The money earned is also used to host workshops, groups and community building activities. At the heart of it all are their monthly club nights, which are some of the most liberated, diverse and straight-up brilliant parties in London. People get down to hip hop, have fierce voguing battles to experimental house music and, most importantly, are respectful,

open and kind to one another. Yes, it's still a night out in London, but Pxssy Palace is also an opportunity to lift up and celebrate marginalised communities by giving QTIPOC (queer, trans, intersex people of colour) space for self-expression without fear of retribution.

QUEER BRUK
instagram.com/queerbruk

Described as London's 'duttiest Queer POC night', Queer Bruk was started by Akeil Onwukwe-Adamson out of a desire to create more spaces that celebrate QTIPOC. Playing a mix of dancehall, afrobeats, soca and more, the night allows people to dance without prejudice, and since its inception in 2018 has developed a community of loyal fans. Onwukwe-Adamson even has dreams of taking Queer Bruk to Notting Hill Carnival. 'I just want to be part of making more space for queer people of colour everywhere,' he told *Hunger* magazine.

R&SHE
randsheclub.com

For a long time, there were hardly any queer clubs or parties for R&B and hip-hop lovers. R&SHE was formed to rectify that. Launched in 2012, the night plays only the best old school R&B, hip hop, '90s classics and floor fillers by female artists only. Starting out as a party held by DJs Neil Prince, David Oh and QBoy in a basement in Dalston for their mates, the night has grown exponentially, travelling as far as New York, LA and Berlin. Now, once a month in East London, R&SHE draws a diverse group of LGBTQ+ folk (and even some straight allies) to their parties, which play tunes from the likes of Cardi B, Aaliyah, Brandy and Mariah Carey.

CENTRAL

THE BUNKER

thebunker.london

Nearest Tube: Baker Street

Not to be confused with the cruise club in East London, the Bunker is an appointment-only dungeon housed in an authentic World War 2 bunker. The location is unknown unless you book, although it's somewhere between Baker Street and Marylebone. Open 24 hours a day, seven days a week, and available to book for a minimum of 90 minutes and up to 12 hours, the Bunker has a full-stocked kit list, including an electronic hoist, a fisting bench, an isolation cell, a St. Andrew's Cross and something described as a 'custom fuck bed'. There are also things like floggers, crops and paddles that visitors can use. You can book the dungeon through the website or by emailing info@thebunker.london.

COVENT GARDEN HEALTH SPA

29 Endell St, West End, WC2H 9BA

cghspa.uk

Nearest Station: Covent Garden

One of the few gay saunas remaining in central London, Covent Garden Health Spa opened in 1985 and was refurbished in 2017. It offers all your usual steam, spa and sexy time, plus a professional massage service and an in-house barber, in case you need a shave before you sauna. A fully licensed bar is on hand to provide Dutch courage for any shrinking violets; bring a print-out of the flyer from the website for a free drink.

PORTSEA SAUNA

2 Portsea Pl, St George's Fields, W2 2BL

gaysaunabar.com

Nearest Tube: Marble Arch

Tucked between Marble Arch and Paddington, Portsea Sauna is a small, discreet space housed in what used to be a beauty parlour, boasting a steam room, dry sauna, backroom, lounge, professional masseurs and a bar. Attracting a slightly older crowd, as well as suited gentleman, this is a friendly place to relax, have fun and meet some like-minded guys.

SWEATBOX

Ramillies House, 1-2 Ramillies St, W1F 7LN

sweatboxsoho.co.uk

Nearest Tube: Piccadilly Circus

Work out then make out together at Sweatbox, Soho's premiere (and only) gay sauna and gym. You'll find everything here: a fully equipped gym, a steam room, a huge jacuzzi, some darkrooms, private cabins, a lounge and massage services. Ever wanted to use a stepper machine starkers? You can at the Naked Workout, which takes place every Sunday. There are also foam parties every weekend, with free entry for under 25s on Mondays and Thursdays. On those days, Sweatbox offers STI screenings by the sexual health savants from Dean Street Express and GMI Partnership. The team from 56 Dean Street also dispense PrEP on Tuesdays to eligible participants who are under-25.

EAST

800 CLUB
800 Lea Bridge Rd, E17 9DN
legs800club.co.uk
Nearest Tube: Walthamstow Central

This three-floored sauna-cum-café-cum-bar has a darkroom, dungeon, steamroll, video lounge and private rooms. It's entirely discreet (we're talking blacked-out windows) and on Thursdays and Saturdays the space mutates into Legs 800, a night for transvestites, trans women and their admirers.

E15 CLUB
6 Leytonstone Rd, E15 1SE
e15club.com
Nearest Tube: Stratford

Close to the Olympic Stadium and Westfield shopping centre, this sauna isn't as popular as Sailors, nor as slick as Sweatbox. Still, it does offer something for East End lads looking to relax, socialise and have a bit of fun. Opened in 2002, there's a jacuzzi, dry sauna, a video lounge and private, lockable rooms, as well as a darkened basement where you'll find beds and other playful accoutrements. Look out for promotions and themed events, like Bear Day.

SAILORS SAUNA
570-574 Commercial Rd, Limehouse, E14 7JD
sailorssauna.com
Nearest Tube: Limehouse Overground/DLR

Previously a part of the now shrunken Chariots gay sauna empire, Sailors is one of London's friendlier saunas, offering a little extra alongside its steamy sessions. Housed next to The White Swan and open to all men – bisexual, gay, questioning and trans – it's on the pricey side, as it doesn't offer the luxury of similar offerings in central London. Still, there's a lot to enjoy: a 20-man hot tub, steam and sauna rooms, private cubicles, a group room and even a roof terrace, should you want to top up your tan. On Mondays you'll find Big-n-Cuddly, a day for larger gentlemen, while on Thursdays Latinx people get discounted entry. There are also the usual deals for under 25s. Sailors differentiates itself by offering food. Fridays is East End Chippy Night, while on Sundays there's a complimentary buffet. You can even order yourself a full English breakfast – handy on Fridays and Saturdays, when Sailors stays open all night.

CRUISING IN LONDON

Despite what some may think, queer Londoners still have an appetite for public sex. While Grindr and other hook-up apps have made sex more immediate and accessible, cottaging (anonymous sex in a public place, usually a lavatory) and cruising still happen all over the city. In the 17th and 18th centuries, Hyde Park and St James's Park were popular cruising grounds, as was the south side of Finsbury Square, which gained the moniker 'Sodomite's Walk'. Men were even known to pick each other up for sex at St Paul's Cathedral.

This tradition never stopped. In the 1930s, while homosexuality was still illegal, the book *For Your Convenience* by Paul Pry, a pseudonym for the author Thomas Burke, provided gay men with a comprehensive guide to the city's public lavatories. Taking the form of a conversation between two men at a gentleman's club, the book details where 'relief' may be found, while the book's endpapers acted as a map. Even after the partial decriminalisation of homosexuality, cottaging and cruising remained popular.

Today, Hampstead Heath and Clapham Common are probably the city's most famous cruising grounds. Both spots are fairly safe, and the police tend to leave people to their own devices – although there's always a risk. Epping Forest is another hot spot, as is Abney Park Cemetery in Stoke Newington and Hyde Park (though its central location makes it popular with tourists and police). The loos at London's train terminals are known to draw men looking for sex, although there has been an attempt to clamp down on such behaviour, and, given that public sex is still illegal in the UK, the un-discreet risk a charge for 'outraging public decency'. Similarly, the public toilets in Soho, once thronging with men, are now heavily policed. There are a few websites that provide information about cottaging and cruising grounds throughout the city, including thegayuk.com and pinkuk.com, and London is home to numerous saunas and cruising bars. Plus, there are no rules that say you can't use Grindr to find where men in your area may be congregating – just remember to stay safe and have fun.

GENTLEMEN

SOUTH END GREEN NW3

The Gentlemen's toilet at South End Green.

LONDON'S MOLLY HOUSES

Before the dawn of the gay bar, queer men in London used to get their kicks at the city's molly houses. The term 'molly' described both female sex workers and effeminate men who engaged in sexual acts with other men. During the late 17th and 18th centuries, molly houses were places where such men could socialise, drink, dance and have sex in relative safety. Given that sodomy in this period was a capital offence under the Buggery Act of 1533, these clandestine meeting points were often located in London's more downtrodden areas, where crime was rife. They could be anywhere, from a tavern to someone's home. Like today's queer clubs, they were subversive. You'd find men wearing women's clothing while engaged in amorous acts, or people going through faux marriage ceremonies (although the sentiments and emotions behind these services may very well have been real) – even fake births with midwives and wooden dolls. The mollies adopted fabulous alter-egos, with names like Plump Nelly, Primrose Mary, Aunt England and, most notably, Princess Seraphina, the alias of butcher John Cooper, who was known to wear her feminine identity out and about in Vauxhall.

Molly houses weren't immune to outside interference. There was always a risk that one could be caught and blackmailed. Likewise, informants let authorities know where molly houses operated and who frequented them. Formed in 1691 with the aim to put an end to immorality, profanity and lewd behaviours (including sex work and sodomy), the Society for the Reformation of Manners policed London's streets, organising raids on establishments they deemed unworthy. The most famous raid occurred in 1726, at one of the most well-known molly houses, Mother Clap's in Holborn. Mother Clap was actually a sympathetic married woman named Margaret Clap, who went above and beyond for her guests. The raid resulted in five men being brought to trial, three of whom were sentenced to death. Mother Clap, also found guilty of disrepute, was sentenced to the pillory in Smithfield, a fine and two years in prison.

The public nature of this trial lead to widespread outrage and moral panic about the debauched and devilish molly houses – not that such scrutiny tempered the mollies. In an 1810 raid at the White Swan on Vere Street, a group of 30 men, later known as the Vere Street Coterie, were arrested for sodomy and attempted sodomy. Eight people were eventually tried, two of whom were sentenced to death. The raids and the risk of arrest grew more serious. By the mid 19th century, the molly houses had been pushed further underground.

HAMPSTEAD HEATH, HIGHGATE MEN'S POND AND KENWOOD LADIES' POND

Hampstead Heath is often dubbed the cruising capital of the world. So popular is the Heath for those seeking sex that in 2006 the *Independent* reported that the City of London spent £40,000 removing condoms and other sex-related waste from the area. It's not exactly clear how long queer folks (and some heterosexual thrill seekers) have been utilising the 790-acre park as a sexual supermarket, although in his book, *Queer City* (Chatto & Windus, 2017), Peter Ackroyd acknowledges that the Heath has long been 'a *locus amoenus* for queer Londoners who found the combination of bushes, trees and long frame irresistible'.

Most cruising takes place on the West Heath, which is separated from the main thrust of the park by North End Way and Spaniards Road, with the main entrance found behind the Jack Straws Castle apartments near the roundabout. Over the years, the police presence here has significantly diminished. While there is, naturally, a risk of being caught, everyone, including neighbours and dog walkers, are aware of what goes on. Indeed, dog walking is a good cover for those who wish to be discreet, be it because they're straight, not out or married. However, people do genuinely use the space to walk their dogs, despite its popularity for public sex – so just be conscious of that if you're venturing up the Heath during the day. Things get busier at night, especially during the summer months when the evenings are long (although Christmas Day is rumoured to be very popular).

Hampstead's queer appeal isn't limited to screwing among the shrubbery: the Highgate Men's Bathing Pond has long been popular with gay men, as anyone who's read a book by Alan Hollinghurst will know. In the '80s and '90s it was a known pick-up spot for guys, and the area remains cruisy to this day, with muscled men showing off in their speedos. Likewise, the grassy bank adjacent to the pond fills up with gay men in the summer months. Like with the West Heath, discretion is advised. This is still a public space, and while the gays might converge there, the law (unfortunately) still applies. There is a nudist area, but it's not all that.

The Kenwood Ladies' Pond has a less playful reputation. While it definitely draws lesbians, it's not cruisy in the same way as the men's pond– which isn't to say naughtiness doesn't occur. Most recently though, the pond was at the centre of the UK's toxic transphobic rhetoric. Trans women were able to use ladies' ponds already, under the Equality Act of 2010 – but the City of London Corporation (CoLC) announced a new gender identity policy, which would ensure that trans women had the right to use the Kenwood Ladies' Pond. Despite protests from transphobic individuals, the policy was upheld, with the Kenwood Ladies' Pond Association saying, 'The Ladies' Pond is a single-sex space and the KLPA is committed to helping to create there an inclusive environment for all women, including transgender women, which is free from discrimination, harassment or victimisation.'

In the words of the late George Michael, who was very fond of the Heath, it's a favourite 'if you're looking for fast love'. In fact, if you want to pay tribute to Michael (who was once arrested in the loos on the Heath) keep an eye out for 'This is My Culture', a party on the West Heath that celebrates the life of the singer and his love of cruising.

Grindr might have made sex readily available, but cruising offers something different, something more physical. So, let's go outside.

The Highgate Men's Bathing Pond, one of London's most beloved open-air swimming pools, has operated for over 150 years.

SOUTH

CHARIOTS VAUXHALL
63 Albert Embankment, Vauxhall, SE1 7TP
chariots.co.uk
Nearest Tube: Vauxhall

For two decades, the Chariots empire ruled London's sauna scene. Opened initially in Shoreditch in 1996, the brand expanded over the next 10 years, with outposts in Limehouse, Streatham, Farringdon, Waterloo and Vauxhall. Done up in mock imitation of a Roman spa, Chariots Shoreditch was the biggest sauna in the UK, sprawling over 20,000 square feet and three floors. Like so many gay venues, it fell victim to gentrification, rising rents, the proliferation of Grindr and redevelopment. In 2016, the site closed, with plans for a hotel to be built in its place. The same fate befell the branches in Streatham, Farringdon (thanks Crossrail) and Waterloo, which was knocked down in 2017. Chariots Limehouse reverted back to its previous name, Sailors, and was sold to a new owner.

Now, all that remains is Vauxhall. Housed under the railway arches, this is the largest sauna in London. It's busy most of the time, especially on the weekends as people mosey in and out of nearby venues like the RVT, the Eagle and Fire. There are 500 lockers, two huge steam rooms, two large saunas, a couple of darkrooms, a maze and 50 private cabins. While it's retained some of the brand's faux-Roman decal, it's more austere than nearby Pleasuredrome, and has slightly shorter opening hours, although it's still open late and non-stop on the weekends (Sunday mornings when the clubs let out are particularly popular). If you want more privacy, you can rent one of the 38 rest rooms for up to 30 minutes, and unlike other spots, this luxury is included in the entrance fee.

This isn't the chattiest of saunas (in fact, talking is actively discouraged). But the atmosphere is friendly and accommodating: if you want to walk around starkers, that's your prerogative, though guests can wear swimming trunks if they prefer. It might be the last stalwart of a former empire, but like the Colosseum in Rome, it retains its historic allure.

THE LOCKER ROOM SAUNA
6 Cleaver St, Prince's, SE11 4DP
lockerroomsauna.co.uk
Nearest Tube: Kennington

Allegedly London's longest running sauna, this place isn't as plush as nearby Pleasuredrome, favouring those who like their sex a little sleazy. There's the usual bits and bobs: a 15-man sauna, showers and ten relaxation cabins (some of which have glory holes and one that boasts a sling). The Locker Room operates different themed nights throughout the week: Mondays is bear night, while every 1st and 3rd Friday is Bi Bi Baby, an inclusive event for men and women who identify as bisexual (although all bi-friendly folks are welcome). There are nights for those into older and younger men, naked nights (which seems obvious) and even fetish parties. It's free for under-25s on Tuesdays.

PLEASUREDROME
Arch, 124 Cornwall Rd, Bishop's, SE1 8XE
pleasuredrome.com
Nearest Tube: Waterloo

Pleasuredrome might be London's slickest sauna. Opened in 1996, this luxurious men-only spa prides itself on being a destination for London's sex-positive scene. Unlike many other saunas, Pleasuredrome is popular with a younger crowd, especially on a Saturday night. It's open 24/7, which helps, and there's a fully licensed bar, so people looking for a sexier alternative to a night on the town are more than catered for. It's also huge. Along with the biggest gay pool spa in London, it boasts two steam rooms, two darkrooms, a maze, a tanning shower, a cinema, and changing room with loads of lockers. The cabins don't offer much privacy or comfort, so if you're looking for something luxe with a lock on the door, you'll want to invest in a deluxe pod. It's £8 for two hours and you get a mattress, pillows, towels and your own TV. In 2020, the place underwent a makeover that would leave Linda Barker jealous with a remodelled bar, refreshed relaxation areas, and better pods and rooms, as well as all-new steam rooms, saunas and spa showers.

Saunas like Chariots Vauxhall promise a steamy end to any night on the town.

CHARIOTS HEALTH SPA
CHARIOTS
chariots.co.uk
Fire exit
Keep clear
Fire exit
Keep clear
CHARIOTS
020 7735 6709
Zone
ENDS
CYCLES ONLY

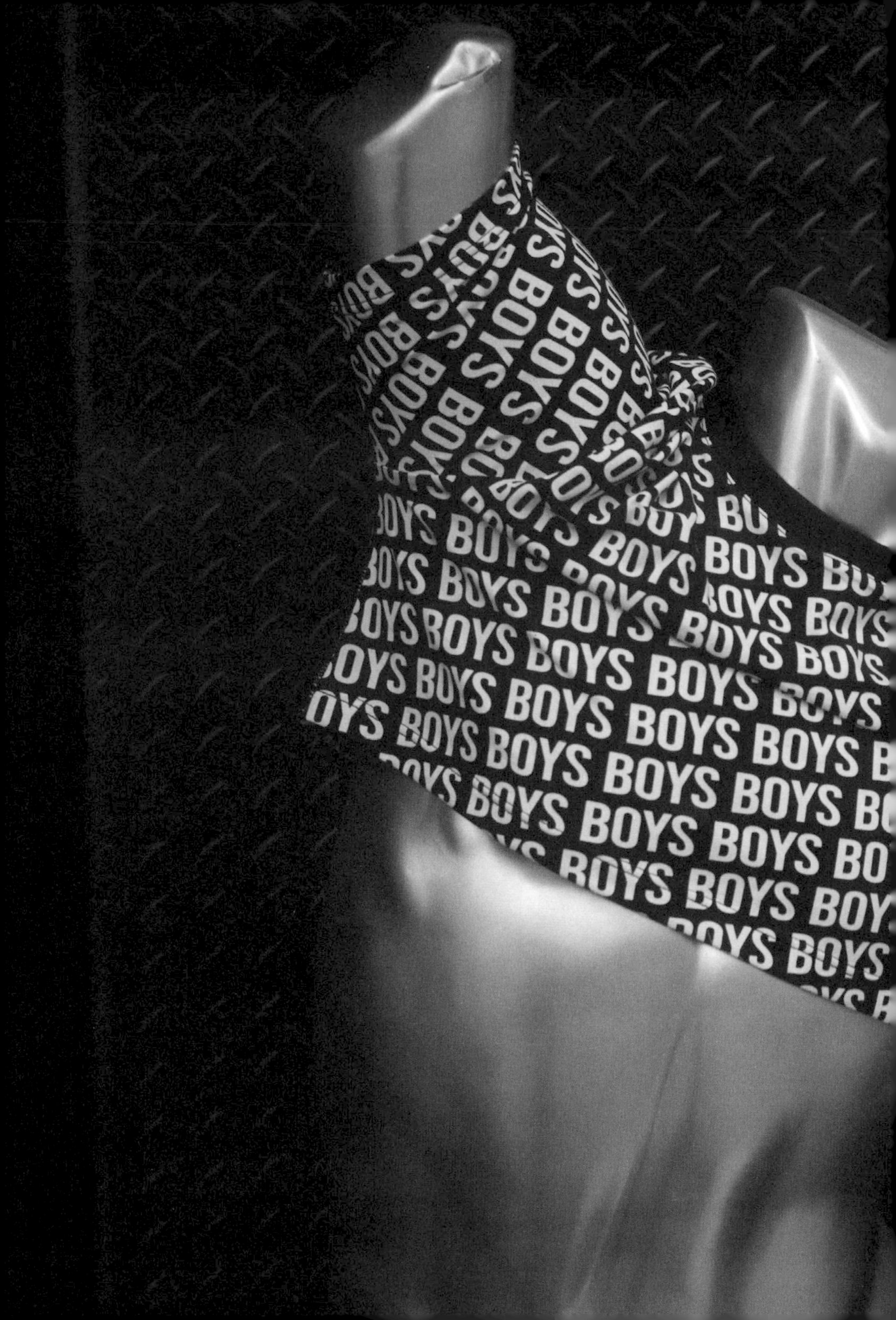
BOYS

SHOPS

CENTRAL

CLONEZONE SOHO

35 Old Compton St, Soho, W1D 5JX
clonezonedirect.co.uk
Nearest Tube: Tottenham Court Road

Serving the LGBTQ+ community for over 30 years, Clonezone is one of London's premiere gay shops. This two-storey Soho flagship store, opened in 2012, sells everything from undies to adult toys. Open until 8pm, keeping up with those who roam Soho by night, it often hosts in-store events, with a full calendar during Pride.

GAY'S THE WORD

66 Marchmont St, Saint Pancras, WC1N 1AB
gaystheword.co.uk
Nearest Tube: Russell Square

For many, there is no queer London without Gay's The Word. Up until recently, it was the UK's only LGBTQ+ bookstore, and has been a community hub for over 40 years. Located on charming Marchmont Street, just south of Euston station, this small but mighty shop houses more queer literature than it would be possible to read in a lifetime. The staff – Jim, Uli and Erica – are immensely knowledgeable about their stock, as well as the wider queer canon. Unsure what you're looking for? They'll help you find it. And if they don't have it, they'll order it. In-store sections include: gay, lesbian, bisexual and trans literature, young adult, non-fiction, poetry, second hand and new releases. They also stock DVDs, magazines, merchandise and journals, and regularly host book launches and author signings,

as well as reading groups and other literary events. For timid teenagers, this bookshop offers a safe, queer environment to ask questions and discover literature, while for older queer folk it's an accessible space that isn't centred around club and bar culture. The staff are welcoming and warm, and provide a fair bit of emotional support to their customers; it's not unheard of for the shop to close early so they can help someone in need. Just as essential today as when it opened over 40 years ago, Gay's The Word is the beating heart of London's LGBTQ+ scene.

PROWLER SOHO

5-7 Brewer St, Soho, W1F 0RF
prowler.co.uk
Nearest Tube: Piccadilly Circus

Founded back in 1989, Prowler began life as a publisher of LGBTQ+ magazines. The first store opened in 1997, and has since become one of the country's main gay retailers. Nowadays, the emphasis has shifted from publishing – although you can still buy books, comics and magazines at this flagship store and online – to adult toys, DVDs, fetish and bondage gear, clothing, club wear, lubes, stimulants and 'aromas' (a.k.a. poppers). There are outlets up and down the UK, as well as a smaller boutique on nearby Old Compton Street (see below).

PROWLER RED

50 Old Compton Street, W1D 4UB

prowler.co.uk

Nearest Tube: Tottenham Court Road

A boutique offshoot just around the corner from Prowler's flagship Soho store, with a focus on fetish and bondage gear.

NORTH

HOUSMANS BOOKSHOP

5 Caledonian Rd, King's Cross, N1 9DY

housmans.com

Nearest Tube: King's Cross St Pancras

Opened in 1945 by writer and playwright Laurence Housman, this is one of the UK's biggest and best radical alternative book stores. Housmans moved to their Caledonian Road space in 1958. They became a central meeting point for the nuclear disarmament movement in the late '50s/'60s, as well as (briefly) for the Gay Liberation Front. In 1974, the London Lesbian & Gay Switchboard (now the charity Switchboard) was founded here. Run from a room above the shop, it provided information and support for LGBTQ+ people, as well as signposting the capital's burgeoning gay scene. Switchboard eventually outgrew Housmans, although they weren't the last to utilise its space, and the bookstore remains a hub for LGBTQ+ people. They have a diverse selection of queer literature, as well as obscure journals and pamphlets, and books on subjects ranging from feminism, racism and environmentalism to the occult; from Foucault to fantasy. Their calendar is constantly packed with literary events, talks, debates and readings, and if you're looking to join a book club there are plenty to consider, including the Feminist Sci-Fi Book Club, Housmans' Queer Book Club, a Black women's reading group and Fuse, which is more generalised. Whatever you're after, as long as it's progressive, radical and aligns with the notions of non-violence and peace, Housmans will have it. If not, they'll get it for you.

GAY'S THE WORD

Established by three gay men, Ernest Hole, Peter Dorey and Jonathan Cutbill, Gay's The Word began its life as a transient bookshop and mail-order service. Inspired by the Oscar Wilde Memorial Bookshop in New York, Hole – with the financial help of Dorey – began roaming London's queer scene selling books. After Hole set up shop at a week-long festival organised by Gay Sweatshop, an LGBTQ+ theatre company, and Gay News, the decision was made: the capital needed a permanent retail space for gay and lesbian literature.

As Camden Council had some empty shops on Marchmont Street, Hole put in a lease application, which ultimately went ignored. It wasn't until he reached out to Ken Livingston (then a councillor) that his request was granted. Along with his partner, Steve Martin, and their white Pyrenean Mountain Dog, Oscar, they moved into 66 Marchmont Street. Hole transformed the space, establishing a cosy café and lining the walls with bookshelves, which overflowed with all the gay and lesbian literature he could get his hands on. The name of the shop was pilfered from a musical written by Ivor Novello. Success was swift: on Thursday nights, cabaret performer Mark Bunyan would commandeer the shop's piano; and the year the bookshop opened, they led the London Gay Pride march.

The shop soon became a community hub, a role it still plays today. Various political and activist groups utilised the space for meetings, including the Gay Black Group and the Lesbian Discussion Group, the latter of which still meets at the shop. By 1983, activist Paud Hegarty was employed here, and Gay's The Word began hosting meetings with Lesbians and Gays Support the Miners a year later: a socialist fundraising and activist group who were assisting those taking part in the miners' strike (see page 125).

That year also saw the bookshop encounter some difficulties. As few gay and lesbian titles were published in the UK, much of their stock was imported from the United States. In April 1984, the shop was raided by HM Customs and Excise, who

believed Gay's The Word was importing and selling pornographic material. Known as Operation Tiger, thousands of pounds of stock was seized, including books by Tennessee Williams, Gore Vidal, Christopher Isherwood, Jean-Paul Sartre and Jean Genet, and the shop's directors were charged with conspiracy to import indecent books, a Victorian law dating back to 1876. The community rallied around the shop, as did a number of writers. A defence fund was launched, with Vidal himself donating £3,000. By this point, the raid had garnered the attention of the press, and newspapers began circulating stories about the associated legal issues. In 1986, two years after the raid, all charges against Gay's The Word's directors were dropped and the case discarded.

In 1989, Jim MacSweeney (pictured, page 103), joined the staff. An associate of the bookshop for over thirty years, he was taken under Hegarty's wing. MacSweeney first visited the shop in 1983 for Ice Breakers, a gay socialist group. It was through them that he first met Hegarty, a political activist who also knew a great deal about books. While Gay's The Word had always been a home to radical political groups, Hegarty's management saw the shop construct a keen political and academic identity, stocking books that fit that remit, as well as fiction. When Hegarty stepped down in 1997, MacSweeney was eager to continue his legacy. Sadly, Hegarty died in 2000 from AIDS-related complications. 'For me, Paud's essence is still in the bookshop,' said MacSweeney, during a panel celebrating 40 years of Gay's The Word in 2020.

In 2007, thanks to rising rents, falling sales and a looming global recession, the shop came under threat of closure. A campaign was launched, with numerous authors and writers, including Ali Smith, Edmund White and Sarah Waters, voicing their support and love for the store. Needing to raise £20,000, people were offered the chance to sponsor a shelf. 'It's a case of use us or lose us,' MacSweeney said to The Times. Thankfully, the shop was saved, and following the release of the film Pride in 2014, Gay's The Word has seen something of a resurgence. 'A whole new generation of people have found the shop for the first time and have come in,' MacSweeney said on a panel. 'And in my 30 years, I have never seen it so busy.'

Social media has also helped Gay's The Word to grow, as well as support from various London-based LGBTQ+ groups, cementing the shop's role as a focal point for the community. The shop still encounters difficulties: like the occasional brick through the window, and a 2020 break-in. The robbers were caught after getting distracted by tequila and prosecco in the shop's basement, and Gay's the Word – resilient to the last – re-opened the very next day.

Nowadays, Gay's The Word is the premiere spot in the city for LGBTQ+ literature. They host a number of author events, talks, signings and meet ups, including the Lesbian Discussion Group and TransLondon, a discussion and support group for all members of the trans community. As writer and historian Neil McKenna said: 'Gay's the Word is a bookshop run by us, for us, an undiluted living archive of queer thought and imagination. Like a friend who always stands by our side and encourages us on, there is a reason why the bookshop is regularly described as a haven, as a sanctuary.' Like so many queer spaces, Gay's the Word is a genuine survivor, weathering not only homophobia, bigotry and hatred, but also London's insatiable appetite for change. This isn't just a bookshop: it's a physical embodiment of queer London.

EAST

GEAR

75 Great Eastern St, Hackney, EC2A 3HN
gearlondon.co.uk
Nearest Tube: Old Street/Shoreditch
High Street Overground

Expectations, an East London fetish shop, serviced the area's leather daddies for 40 years before closing in 2016. In its place grew Gear, a London offshoot of the luxury Berlin fetish outfitters from Rob Dilly and Matthias Kaminsky. While on the expensive side, this uber-trendy sex shop sells everything you can imagine, from lubes and adult toys to waterproof sheets and gimp masks. But it's the designer gear and leathers that really sets it apart, stocking the likes of RoB London, Langlitz Leather, Blackstyle and even Adidas.

SH! WOMEN'S EROTIC EMPORIUM

31-35 Pitfield Street, Hoxton, N1 6HB
sh-womenstore.com
Nearest Tube: Old Street

Sh! was the UK's first sex shop to cater specifically to women. Opened in 1992 by Ky Hoyle as an alternative to the then-seedy sex shops of Soho, Sh! puts women's pleasure first. Initially, men weren't allowed inside. That policy has changed, though men must still be accompanied by a woman, to keep the space safe and welcoming. Sh! started manufacturing their own sex toys, including dildos, strap-ons and bondage gear; and can claim to their fame that they popularised the rabbit vibrator. The brand works collaboratively with the NHS regarding women's sexual health, and moved from Hoxton Square to their current address on Pitfield Street in 2017. There's a café on the new premises, so you can grab a bite and a bullet vibe in one visit. Perfect.

MUNROE BERGDORF

As Black trans woman, Munroe Bergdorf acknowledges that her body and identity has always been politicised. From the moment she realised she had a platform, she poured her energy and soul into advocating for the most marginalised groups in society, particularly queer, transgender, non-binary and intersex people of colour. Born in 1987, she grew up in Stansted Abbotts, a majority white area on the borders of Hertfordshire and Essex, with a Jamaican father and a white, English mother. At the all-boys school she attended, she was mercilessly bullied for being effeminate, even facing violence from her classmates. By the time she went to university in Brighton to study English, she had begun exploring her gender identity, wearing makeup and high heels. She began her transition aged 24 – while teaching herself to DJ, on the side. Soon after, she started modelling, working with brands like Illamasqua and Boy London, and got involved with clubnight Pxssy Palace. Munroe fell into activism after she took part in a Uniqlo campaign in 2016, where she was asked to speak about her experiences as a Black, trans person. She soon began to speak out on social media about her experiences with racism and transphobia.

In 2017 she made history, becoming the first trans model to front a L'Oréal campaign in the UK. However, an apparent smear campaign led by right-wing media misinterpreted comments Munroe made regarding the realities of systemic racism. L'Oréal dropped her from the campaign, a move widely criticised by LGBTQ+ people and people of colour. As a result, Munroe experienced a deluge of horrific transphobia and racism. Nevertheless, she has said that what came out of the experience 'has been greater than what it was intended to be in the first place'. Later that year, she became the face of UK-based beauty brand, Illamasqua, and in 2018 she made a documentary with Channel 4, *What Makes A Woman*, which explored gender identity. She was awarded an honorary doctorate by the University of Brighton in 2019 for her tireless campaigning for transgender rights, and was appointed as a UN Women UK Changemaker in 2020. That same year, L'Oréal Paris apologised to Munroe and she joined the company's UK diversity and inclusion advisory board. Appearing regularly in publications like *i-D*, *Glamour*, *Paper* and *Vogue*, Munroe recently signed a six-figure deal for her debut book, *Transitional*, which is set for release in 2021.

HEALTH AND
COMMUNITY

CENTRAL

NORTH

HEALTH

HEALTH

56 DEAN STREET
56 Dean St, Soho, W1D 6AQ
dean.st
Nearest Tube: Leicester Square Station

56 Dean Street is the largest sexual health and wellbeing clinic in London. They specialise in the testing, treatment and prevention of HIV. In the early 1980s it was part of Westminster Hospital, known as Outpatient 6, before moving to Vincent Square. It wasn't until 2009 that this unit found its home in Dean Street.

In 2003, this became the first NHS service to offer rapid HIV Point of Care testing. They set the world record for the number of HIV tests performed in one location in 2011 (at G-A-Y, FYI). In 2011, the NHS opened Dean Street Express at number 34, the first sexual health clinic with an infinity machine, which delivered test results within six hours.

Today, along with sexual health screenings, Dean Street offer specific services for trans and non-binary folk, counselling, advice regarding PrEP and PEP, outpatient care for people living with HIV, and chemsex support. With a particular understanding and focus on the LGBTQ+ community, sex work, drug taking and wider societal discrimination, Dean Street has a unique and holistic approach to sexual health and wellbeing.

GENDER IDENTITY CLINIC
Lief House, 3 Sumpter Close,
Finchley Road, NW3 5HR
gic.nhs.uk
Nearest Tube: Finchley Road

The Gender Identity Clinic has been operating since 1966, making it the oldest gender clinic in the UK. They provide a number of different services and holistic gender care, with an emphasis on the biological, medical, psychological and social aspects of gender.

GENDER IDENTITY DEVELOPMENT SERVICE
The Tavistock Centre, 120 Belsize Lane, NW3 5BA
gids.nhs.uk
Nearest Tube: Finchley Road

Colloquially known as the Tavistock gender clinic, this is the UK's only gender identity service specialising in children. Operating since 1989, it has posts in London and Leeds, as well as various outreach clinics. It provides assessments, support, physical interventions, groups and family days, which normalise gender variance in a safe space and give family members the chance to explore their feelings.

EAST

COMMUNITY

HEALTH

THE CROSSROADS WOMEN'S CENTRE
25 Wolsey Mews, Kentish Town, NW5 2DX
crossroadswomen.net
Nearest Tube: Kentish Town

MILDMAY MISSION HOSPITAL
19 Tabernacle Gardens, E2 7DZ
mildmay.org
Nearest Tube: Hoxton Overground Station

Beginning its life as a squat near Euston Station, the Crossroads Women's Centre was started by the Wages for Housework Campaign in 1975. A number of women's groups started using the space, including Black Women for Wages for Housework, the English Collective of Prostitutes, Wages Due Lesbians, and Women Against Rape. After a move in 1978, a run-down shop on Tonbridge Street became the King's Cross Women's Centre. Here, conferences were held, including the 1989 campaign 'Who Works for Me?', an anti-racist and anti-sexist project that saw students from over 20 inner-city schools exploring the labour – emotional, physical and caring – that the women in their lives did for them, their families and communities. In 1997, the group moved to Kentish Town and rebranded as the Crossroads Women's Centre. Today, the organisation offers a safe space for women escaping racial, anti-migrant, domestic and sexual violence. They host workshops, film screenings, exhibitions and social events.

The Mildmay Mission was formed in the mid-1860s by Reverend William Pennefather, to provide spiritual guidance and care to the sick. After the cholera outbreak in 1866, Mildmay's small team of nurses expanded to the Mildmay Mission Hospital, which operated out of a disused warehouse from 1892. After the formation of the NHS in 1948, the validity of the hospital was brought under question, and by the mid '80s, with only 200 beds, the hospital was deemed 'uneconomical' and closed down.

Despite this, Mildmay's Trustee Board, led by Helen Taylor Thompson, fought for the hospital's survival. It reopened in 1988 as the first hospice in Europe for those living with HIV and fighting AIDS-related illnesses. At the time, effective antiretroviral therapies had yet to become widely available, and HIV/AIDS treatment involved palliative care. While people would receive acute treatment and care at the Broderip Ward at the Middlesex Hospital, the UK's first ward dedicated to HIV patients, Mildmay offered a more holistic approach, such as hospice care for those at the end of their lives. The hospital made the headlines after receiving numerous visits from Princess Diana. Her proximity to the patients helped reduce some of the stigma attached to HIV/AIDS.

Advances in the treatment of HIV/AIDS meant that, over the years, Mildmay's focus moved away from hospice care. They have become Europe's only centre dedicated to the rehabilitation of people living with HIV-Associated Neurocognitive Disorders (HAND), although they still provide inpatient and day-care services. In 2015, new, purpose-built hospital facilities were constructed, with Prince Harry, continuing his mother's efforts, officially opening the building. However, in early 2020 it was revealed that Mildmay faced closure following budget cuts to services by the Conservative government. During the COVID-19 pandemic, one of the hospital's two wards began to provide a step-down service for patients with coronavirus, with a focus primarily on patients experiencing homelessness, while the other ward continued to provide HIV services. At the time of writing, the long-term fate of Mildmay remains uncertain – although the hospital's Chief Executive, Geoff Coleman, is optimistic. 'The hospital has the opportunity to demonstrate that we can effectively treat patients who are homeless,' he said during a recent Q&A, 'thus opening up a new specialism.' Hopefully, this will be enough to save the Mildmay.

COMMUNITY

EAST END LESBIANS, BI AND QUEER WOMEN
meetup.com/East-End-Lesbians-Bi-and-Queer-Women

Describing themselves as 'a bunch of East End Lezzers, Bi and Queer gals out for fun and trouble', East End Lesbians, Bi and Queer Women is a community group for exactly who it says on the tin. Open to all women of any age, including refugees and asylum seekers, they organise regular meet ups, a book club, workshops, brunches, nights out and dinners. Run entirely by volunteers, if you're up for the task you can also organise events, too. There's only one condition: 'No haters of any variety, ta!'

FRIENDS OF THE JOINERS ARMS
thejoinersliveson.wordpress.com

Founded in 2014, in the run up to the closure of this legendary East London hangout, Friends of the Joiners Arms initially formed to keep the pub open. After the Joiners shut its doors in 2015, the group campaigned to save the pub from developers, who wanted to demolish the site to build luxury housing. In 2017, the group successfully convinced Tower Hamlets council to stipulate that while redevelopment could occur, the new building must include a pub that should be run as an LGBTQ+ venue for at least 25 years, with opening hours that reflected those of the original. The developers would also pay the venue's rent for a year and contribute to the refitting costs. Aiming to become a not-for-profit Community Benefit Society, the Friends put a bid in for the lease of the new venue. There have been developmental delays, however: as of January 2020, the site remains empty, with developers now petitioning Tower Hamlets to transform the space into a hotel. Thankfully, the precondition for an LGBTQ+ pub remains. Entirely community lead, and always looking for new members and volunteers, Friends of the Joiners Arms exemplifies the solidarity, strength and power of London's LGBTQ+ population.

FIRST OUT

First Out was a queer café and bar on St Giles High Street that operated for 25 years. Opened in 1986, it was the first daytime queer commercial venue in London, offering a much-needed alternative to the bar and club scene that had sprouted in late-'80s Earl's Court and Soho. In an era before the internet and social networking, this café provided an essential service for the LGBTQ+ community. While the gay press offered listings and news, First Out had a community noticeboard that allowed people to advertise flat shares, workshops, book groups, performing arts meet-ups and more. They also hosted exhibitions for up-and-coming queer artists, as well as events that showcased LGBTQ+ talent. The café was known to be truly inclusive at a time when London's LGBTQ+ scene was fairly divided, with lesbians, gays, bisexuals, trans people and more all dropping in for a latte, some hummus (the food was vegetarian) or a cocktail in the basement bar. Unfortunately, due to the Crossrail developments and changes in the lease, the owners were forced to close the café in 2011.

HEALTH

CLINIQ

Caldecot Centre, 15-22 Caldecot Rd,
Brixton, SE5 9RS
cliniq.org.uk
Nearest Tube: Denmark Hill Overground

CliniQ was launched in 2012 in partnership with King's College Hospital to provide trans and non-binary people with a specific health care space. Today, it provides free sexual health services and a broader, holistic well-being clinic for trans and non-binary people and their family and friends. This includes counselling, support and advice, acupuncture, yoga and a variety of free sexual health services. There is also peer support, where a team of trans caseworkers, counsellors and advisors from different backgrounds can offer help in a number of different areas, including issues with transitioning, sex and relationships, alcohol and substance use, employment, discrimination, hate crimes and sexual assault.

BLACKOUT UK

blkoutuk.com

BlackOut UK is a community group and collective created to make space for Black gay, bisexual, trans and queer men through discussion, creativity and support. This manifests itself through articles, film, photography, art, meet-ups and more, including their monthly Black Men Who Brunch events. These elevate brunch into an experience, complete with performing arts, skills exchanges, debate and dancing. In 2020, BlackOut UK launched their community mobile app, the BlackOut Hub.

GAY OUTDOOR CLUB

goc.org.uk

Organising more than 500 events each year around the UK, the Gay Outdoor Club boasts over 1,500 members made up of LGBTQ+ folk who enjoy all things outdoorsy. In London, this includes monthly urban walks, trips around the Home Counties and strolls around the many parks in the city. They also offer a number of specialist activities, such as rock climbing, cycling, swimming and even skiing.

GRRRL ZINE FAIR

grrrlzinefair.com

Founded by Lu Williams, a queer, working-class artist from Essex, Grrrl Zine Fair is far more than an indie magazine convention. Imbued with a DIY ethos and mentality, this group platforms women and non-binary artists through a number of live events, gigs, parties, workshops and, of course, zine fairs. Curated by Williams, this includes self-publishing fairs, panel talks, performances, live music and exhibitions. Their own publication, the *Grrrl in Print* zine, is unmissable – as is the feminist zine library, a travelling archive of over 200 feminist and LGBTQ+ zines compiled using donations from zine makers and publications purchased thanks to donations. Grrrl Zine Fair has also appeared at festivals, the V&A and the BFI.

LONDON LESBIAN AND GAY CENTRE

The London Lesbian and Gay Centre lived a short but heady life. Opened officially in 1985 in a former meat warehouse on Cowcross Street, Farringdon, with the assistance of a near £1 million grant from the Greater London Council (led at the time by Ken Livingstone), the centre was the first large-scale LGBTQ+ initiative that any governmental body had put money behind. Spread over five floors, it offered a little bit of everything, from a basement theatre/club and a more accessible café/bar on the ground floor, to a 'women-only' floor. There was space for community meetings and facilities for printing and photography, too.

As the first non-commercial queer space in London, it allowed gay men and lesbians a safe destination to meet at, outside of the bar and club scene. For many, especially young queer people, the Centre was a lifeline. Its novelty, however, was a double-edge sword. Because of the scarcity of such spaces, the organisational body of the centre were, to quote LGBTQ+ activist and the co-founder of Stonewall, Lisa Power, 'total amateurs chosen for their political categories or beliefs and not for being able to run a successful social or commercial undertaking'. Rifts and factions swiftly formed. Bisexual and BDSM groups were banned from the centre, a decision that was overturned just three months later. Similarly, as Power told *Vice*, the 'women-only' floor was selective about the types of lesbians they gave access to. There was a real lack of inclusivity, with some working-class queer folks and queer people of colour feeling ostracised.

In 1986, the Conservative government, led by Prime Minister Margret Thatcher, dissolved the Greater London Council, who owned the building. With the loss of authoritative governmental support, the centre was left unmoored. It soon became apparent that since its inception the centre had been subject to theft and fraud, be it volunteers handing out free food to their friends or bar stock going missing. Thousands of pounds were even stolen from the safe, with insurers refusing to cover the loss as the safe hadn't been forced open.

Ultimately, the infighting among different groups, the lack of a centralised vision, an inability to compromise and huge financial losses and debts resulted in the building being sold in 1991. Still, for just over five years the Centre provided an alternative space for the city's queer community, which initiatives like the proposed London LGBTQ+ Community Centre are attempting to recreate in a more inclusive, professional manner today.

BLACK LESBIAN AND GAY CENTRE

Operating from 1985 to the late 1990s, the Black Lesbian and Gay Centre was an essential resource for London's queer Black community (although it was open to all queer people of colour). Initially based in Tottenham, it moved several times over the years, from Peckham Rye to Westminster Bridge Road. It offered a telephone helpline, support services and a social space, with a large focus on arts programming. It also produced a newsletter, *BlackOut*, copies of which can be found at the Bishopsgate Institute. The centre was the subject of the documentary *Under Your Nose*.

CAMPAIGN FOR HOMOSEXUAL EQUALITY (CHE)

Along with the Gay Liberation Front, the Campaign for Homosexual Equality is one of the oldest LGBTQ+ activist groups in the UK. Its origins date back to 1964, three years before the partial decriminalisation of homosexuality. The organisation took on its current moniker in 1971. Despite being based in Manchester, it maintained its strong connections with London, even organising the 1974 national Homosexual Equality Rally in the city. In 1972, they also opened the CHE London Information Centre, which operated out of a basement on Great Windmill Street in Soho. The main office moved to London in 1979 and various local offshoots formed across the country during the '80s. However, mass-membership dwindled as a result of these splinter groups and various other organisations, such as Stonewall and OutRage!, became more prominent. While still active, as of October 2019 the Executive Committee of CHE had proposed that the organisation be dissolved and that their remaining resources be used 'to document and record the very important part that CHE has played in improving the lives of lesbian and gay people'.

CAMDEN LESBIAN CENTRE AND BLACK LESBIAN GROUP

For nearly 10 years, Camden housed the UK's only dedicated lesbian centre on Phoenix Road. The project was devised by a group of lesbians who met at the Kentish Town Women's Workshop and the Camden Black Lesbian Group, opening their own space in 1987. The centre was home to many groups, including GEMMA, a lesbian disability group; and Zamimass, who advocated for a Black lesbian and gay section on the Pride march. With the arrival of Section 28 and funding issues, the centre was ultimately forced to close in the 1990s – though the Black Lesbian Group continued to operate.

HIGHBURY FIELDS: THE FIRST GAY RIGHTS DEMONSTRATION IN BRITAIN

On 27 November 1970, the Gay Liberation Front organised the first gay rights demonstration in Britain at Highbury Fields. Around 150 activists held a torch-lit rally to protest police brutality against the LGBTQ+ community following the arrest of Louis Eakes, detained for cruising several men in an entrapment operation. 'The GLF protest in November 1970 was a milestone in gay history,' said LGBTQ+ activist Peter Tatchell in 2000. 'For the first time in Britain, gay people demonstrated to demand human rights. Before this protest, the police harassed the gay community with impunity. The 27th November 1970 was the moment that lesbians and gay men got up off their knees. It ended forever the era of queers as passive victims of injustice. From that date onwards, the fear that had cowed gay people into submission was gone. Instead of fear, we felt pride and defiance.' In 2000, a plaque commemorating the event was unveiled.

KENRIC
kenriclesbians.org.uk

Established in 1965, Kenric is the UK's longest running lesbian social group. Its name is a portmanteau of Kensington and Richmond, the areas in London in which their community originated, although a network of other groups have sprouted up all over the UK. Today, most of their events do occur in London, although the *Kenric Magazine*, contact adverts and online services keep the various outliers connected. Most members are aged over 40, and all women, including trans women, are welcome, as long as they identify as a lesbian. social events vary from informal monthly drop-ins, book clubs and museum trips, to their Purple Ribbon Events, large-scale parties with live music, DJs and dancing. Given the lack of offerings specifically for queer women in London, Kenric provides lesbians of all ages with space to connect.

LESBIANS AND GAYS SUPPORT THE MIGRANTS
lgsmigrants.com

Inspired by the story of activist group Lesbians and Gays Support the Miners (see page 125), and galvanised by right-wing anti-migrant demonisations, Lesbians and Gays Support the Migrants formed to stand in solidarity with migrants and refugees. With media and political groups hijacking the fight for LGBTQ+ rights to justify their anti-migrant sentiments, LGSMigrants built on a tradition of radical queer politics that advocates for other marginalised groups in society. Along with fundraising, events and digital activism, LGSMigrants organise direct action and protests, which usually have a theatrical queer spin. These have included burning £35,000 worth of 'Theresa May' money in response to a policy that meant non-EU workers in Britain could be deported if they earned less than £35,000 a year; drag queens delivering letters to airlines calling for them to stop partaking in deportations; hanging a banner reading 'Queer Solidarity Smashes Borders' from Vauxhall Bridge; placing guerrilla adverts on the Tube about how to stop the deportation of migrants; and, in 2019, joining the back of the Pride in London parade alongside the Outside Project and African Rainbow Family, despite not applying for a spot. They host regular open meetings and anyone interested in joining should reach out via social media or email. As they say, 'As queer people, we know what it is like to be labelled illegal. We have experience of being targets for the police and media, and we know what it's like to be scapegoated and turned into objects of hate based on who we are. We think it's crucial to use the experiences of our community to find commonality with those targeted most harshly through state oppression now. We want to use the strength of our queer community to stand in solidarity with groups who are being attacked.'

LONDON LGBTQ+ COMMUNITY CENTRE
londonlgbtqcentre.org

The London LGBTQ+ Community Centre is a community-led project to open a new queer hub in London. Entirely organised by volunteers, in 2018 they successfully crowdfunded £102,000 to get the project off the ground. Their vision for the centre is to create an accessible, multi-purpose not-for-profit space run by and for LGBTQ+ people. Their proposed building will have a café, meeting rooms and co-working spaces, and will act as a multi-generational social centre. They plan to include an information hub

RAILTON ROAD AND THE SOUTH LONDON GAY COMMUNITY CENTRE

In the 1970s and '80s, Brixton was a hotbed of radical queer politics, activism and LGBTQ+ solidarity. Between 1974-1976, the South London Gay Community Centre was the nucleus. Operating out of 78 Railton Road, this building (a squat comprised of an empty shop, a basement and two floors of office space) was filled with queer activity. While gay and lesbian discos had sprouted up in Lambeth, there was a need for more visible, permanent queer spaces. Along with hosting meetings of the South London Gay Liberation Group, an offshoot of the GLF, the centre housed many other activist groups. There was a drop-in café and a telephone help-line, and the basement used to offer discos and film screenings.

The South London Gay Community Centre wasn't alone on Railton Road. There were two women's centres, one of which was next door; the Anarchist News Service; and radical Black collective, Race Today. Alongside these organisations were the residential squats known as the 'Brixton Gay Community': a cluster of houses on Railton and Mayall Road. These buildings backed on to each other, providing the perfect opportunity for an alternative form of living that eroded the notion of private property ownership. Dividing walls were demolished, both in the gardens and the houses themselves. A queer housing network soon developed, where people could come and go. Out of this was born the Brixton Faeries, a political theatre group, whose name was later adopted by the community of activists living in the squats. It's worth noting that the 'Brixton Gay Community' was overwhelmingly made up of cisgender gay men. While three women did live in the squats, a larger lesbian community could be found on nearby Bellefields Road.

In 1976, the centre was evicted. But by that point a community had been established, and all political activity shifted to the squats in Railton and Mayall Road. These squatters were predominantly white, despite Brixton becoming increasingly populated by the Afro-Caribbean community. As a result, a Black gay community rose up in Brixton, developing its own Black gay venues. One of these was a shebeen (an illegal bar or club operating without a licence) run by a middle-aged Jamaican woman named Pearl. 'It wasn't quite "Queer Nation",' wrote Brixton Faerie Terry Stewart, 'but we did enjoy ourselves in an environment that was free from the usual racism that was pretty much run-of-the-mill [...] on the gay scene at the time.'

The Brixton Black Women's Group was one of the first such groups in the UK. Co-founders Olive Morris and Liz Obi squatted at 121 Railton Road. This house became a central spot for political groups such as Black People Against State Harassment, and was home to Sabarr Bookshop, one of the first run for and by the Black community. Sadly, Morris died in 1979 from non-Hodgkins Lymphoma. She was just 26.

After the Sabarr Bookshop relocated in 1980, a local anarchist group moved in. Thus, the 121 Centre was formed. Operating as an anarchist bookshop, the space had a club and a café, utilised by many anarchist and LGBTQ+ groups. In 1999, after months of legal back-and-forth, the squatters were evicted. The 121 Centre was no more.

The Brixton Gay Community had experienced a similar, albeit less dramatic fate. By the 1980s, the squats on Railton Road had fallen into disrepair and, as Matt Cook wrote in his book *Queer Domesticities* (Palgrave Macmillan, 2014), the sense of optimism had gone. The squats were transformed into single-person units, becoming a part of the Brixton Housing Co-operative's gay subgroup. Some residents moved on. The communal gardens were left intact, and the Housing Co-op's policies opened up to lesbians in the '90s.

In the '80s Brixton became popular as a queer nightlife spot, with venues like the Fridge, the Prince of Wales on the corner of Coldharbour Lane (now a giant KFC) and the Loughborough Hotel all catering to the LGBTQ+ community. Unfortunately, none survive. As always, London's queer scene is caught in a state of constant flux.

that can signpost services, including other LGBTQ+ organisations who will be able to make use of clinic and therapy spaces. With the support of the Mayor's office and Hackney Council, the team at the London LGBTQ+ Community Centre have been working consistently to make their vision a reality. They are currently searching for a permanent space in London that fulfils all their needs.

QUEERPACK
queerpack.co

Launched in 2019 by a group of queer twentysomethings who wanted to binge episodes of *The Great British Bakeoff* in company, Queerpack has become an answer to the lack of IRL spaces for LBTQ+ womxn and non-binary people in London. Meeting every Wednesday at various different locations, this group (open to queer women, trans and non-binary folx) now boasts over 100 members, who organise meets at pubs, markets and parks.

QUEERS WITHOUT BEERS
joinclubsoda.com/queers-without-beers

So much of the queer scene revolves around drinking, be it at bars or clubs. Queers Without Beers aims to rectify that. Beginning as a collaboration between Club Soda, the mindful-drinking movement, and charity London Friend in 2016, they arrange monthly alcohol-free events for those looking to socialise without the sauce. Whether you've never been into booze, you're trying to cut down, you don't drink for religious reasons, or have cut alcohol out of your life, Queers Without Beers welcomes all LGBTQ+ people into their sober space. Their London group meets every third Wednesday of the month. A diverse list of drinks is on the menu, including alcohol-free beers and cider, the teetotal GnT and distilled botanical brand Seedlip (nice with tonic, FYI). Filled with a range of people from all age groups, backgrounds, gender identities and sexualities, Queers Without Beers is perfect for those who don't want to drink but who still appreciate a night down the pub.

SOUTHBANK SURFING
facebook.com/groups/southbanksurfing

Southbank Surfing is a regular free meet up for lesbians, bisexual and queer women. Started by Clair and Claire, who usually host the evenings out of a pub in Clerkenwell, the events are attended by loads of women who want to meet like-minded people. With London's lack of a dedicated lesbian scene, events like Southbank Surfing also provide an entry point for those who may not know any other LGBTQ+ people, or who may be intimidated by Soho bars and club nights in East London. Nervous newbies should head down early to meet people before it gets rammed. This'll also give you a chance to ask about the name – given that Southbank Surfing neither takes place on London's Southbank, nor involves surfing…

VOICES4 LONDON
voices4london.org.uk

Voices4 was founded in New York by activist and writer Adam Eli in 2017 as a way for LGBTQ+ people to use their relative privileges to lift up, amplify and support local and global LGBTQ+ activism, be it trans and intersex rights, the marginalisation of queer people of colour, or protesting the persecution of LGBTQ+ people in different countries. The London division was formed in 2019, where they marched behind the official Pride in London parade. Since then they have organised kiss-ins, joined the protests against Boris Johnson and the Conservative government, raised funds for other organisations and marched in solidarity with the trans community at the first Trans+ Pride in London. In the words of their founder: 'Queers anywhere are responsible for queers everywhere.'

WOTEVER WORLD
woteverworld.com

Wotever World is a non-profit organise centred on queer arts and culture. They organise parties, fairs, films, meetings, fundraisers, performances and more. On Tuesdays, they host Bar Wotever at the Royal Vauxhall Tavern, a weekly meet up and variety show for LGBTQ+ people, performers and creatives that has run in some capacity since 2005. Founded by Ingo Cando, Bar Wotever encourages performances from new and established mixed cabaret artists across all intersections of the LGBTQ+ community.

Wotever World organise the Female Masculinity Appreciation Society, an evening that celebrates drag kings, arm wrestling and dancing. They host Non-Binary Cabaret, a celebration of non-binary identities and a lesson on all things gender and sexuality, at various venues around London. You can also find them organising Queer Fayre, a pop-up arts and crafts market and meeting space for LGBTQ+ folk and allies who like to get creative. As per their manifesto, Wotever welcomes everyone: 'this includes, but certainly is not exclusive to: drag kings, trans, queers, non-binary, women, mtf, femmes, trans, butches, gay, drag queens, dykes, bisexuals, ftm, men, straight… Wotever etc. All will respect all.'

GAY LIBERATION FRONT (GLF)

Between 1970-1973, the Gay Liberation Front (GLF) encouraged gay and lesbian people to live their lives openly while challenging discrimination, prejudice and persecution. Established by Bob Mellors and Aubrey Walter who had spent time with the GLF in New York and attended the 'Revolutionary Peoples Constitutional Convention', organised by the Black Panther Party, the first meeting took place at the London School of Economics (LSE), where Mellors was a student. The group was known for being, in the words of member Peter Tatchell, 'feisty, radical and uncompromising'. Their offerings varied from political campaigns and demonstrations to club nights.

In November 1970, the GLF organised the first UK public demonstration by lesbians and gay men at Highbury Fields. The following year, they published the 'Gay Liberation Front Manifesto', which set out key demands and principles for the organisation, as well as describing the ways that lesbians and gay people were oppressed by society. That same year, the GLF invaded the Festival of Light, a conservative, anti-LGBTQ Christian group co-founded by Mary Whitehouse. Members of the GLF released mice, unveiled banners, blew horns and kissed each other while wearing drag. After moving their meeting space to All Saints Church in Notting Hill, the group also successfully fought back against police, who had told local pubs not to serve GLF members.

However, by the end of 1971, the organisational nature of the GLF was fraying, partly due to the diverging social and political ideologies of its members. Splinter groups soon formed, including the GLF Camden and the South London GLF, who held meetings at a squat on Railton Road. Similarly, while the GLF manifesto embraced feminism and aligned itself with women's liberation, the women of the GLF walked out in 1972, with various radical feminist and separatist lesbian groups forming as a result. By the end of 1973, according to LGBTQ+ activist and co-founder of Stonewall, Lisa Power, the GLF was disintegrating. Tensions bubbled over between the conventional organisers and the more radical wing, who had set up a bookshop at a warehouse in Bethnal Green. Members of that group, known as 'Bethnal Rouge', even raided the GLF offices (at that time in Caledonian Road). The offices shut down in February, 1974.

Despite the collapse of GLF, a number of influential organisations grew from their groundwork. These included *Gay News*, Switchboard, gay socialist group IceBreakers, the Brixton Faeries, theatre group Bloolips and OutRage!, who formed in 1990 in response to the murder of gay actor Michael Boothe and included people like Peter Tatchell, an active member of the GLF. As Stuart Feather (the GLF member who founded Bloolips) noted in 2007, the networks and groups that formed because of and out of the Gay Liberation Front became essential during the height of the HIV/AIDS crisis.

In 2020, to celebrate the organisation's 50th anniversary, 12 veterans from the Gay Liberation Front, including Peter Tatchell, marched through London. They followed the route traditionally taken by Pride in London, which was cancelled due to the global COVID-19 pandemic. 'We're here to mark the 50th anniversary of the Gay Liberation Front, which ignited the modern movement for LGBTQ+ riots in Britain,' said Tatchell, at the event. 'And we're also here to reclaim Pride. Pride can be a celebration, but it also must be a march for LGBTQ+ human rights in Britain and around the world. And today, we especially want to extend our solidarity to Black Lives Matter and Black LGBTQ+ people all over the world. We stand with you.'

LESBIANS AND GAYS SUPPORT THE MINERS

Lesbians and Gays Support the Miners (LGSM) were a group of lesbian and gay activists who campaigned and fundraised in solidarity with the National Union of Mineworkers during the UK miners' strike of 1984-85. The group began with just two gay men, Mark Ashton and his friend Mike Jackson, who organised a bucket collection during the Pride march of '84. Soon after, 11 people got together to support the miners. They began fundraising at pubs, bars and outside Gay's The Word bookshop, where they had started to meet. Because the Thatcher government sequestered funds from the National Union of Mineworkers, direct donations to the union became pointless. As a result, it was recommended that supporters build links with specific mining communities, and LGSM forged solidarity links with the South Wales mining communities of Dulais.

Along with sending money to Dulais to help the striking miners and their families, LGSM visited the town of Neath in the Dulais Valley, which helped break down barriers for lesbians and gay people. As both groups faced media persecution, LGBTQ+ people and the miners developed a tenable bond. In November 1984, a splinter group called Lesbians Against Pit Closures was formed to provide a women-only space to organise, although women did remain in LGSM. In December that year, LGSM organised their biggest fundraising event, the 'Pits and Perverts' benefit concert at the Electric Ballroom in Camden. Headlined by Bronski Beat, the event raised £5,650.

The bonds between LGSM and the National Union of Mineworkers also made a space for LGBTQ+ people within the trade union movement. In October 1984 at the Labour Party conference, the National Union of Mineworkers sent a message of solidarity with the Labour Campaign for Lesbian and Gay Rights, leading the party to officially commit to supporting LGBTQ+ rights a year later. In total, LGSM raised approximately £22,500 (around £68,000 by today's standards) for the miners who were on strike and their families.

The National Union of Mineworkers, the mining communities of South Wales and LGSM led the 1985 Pride march in London. LGSM folded soon after. A documentary about the organisation and their work, *All Out! Dancing in Dulais*, was released in 1986. In 2014, the film *Pride* was released, based on these events. That year, LGSM also published *Pride: The Unlikely Story of the True Heroes of the Miner's Strike*, an oral history of their activism. A blue plaque was installed above Gay's The Word bookshop in 2017, celebrating the life of the movement's co-founder Mark Ashton (who died in 1987 of AIDS-related complications) and the work of LGSM.

PETER TATCHELL

For over 50 years, Peter Tatchell has been campaigning for LGBTQ+ rights, social equality and justice. Born in Australia in 1952, he was involved in student activism as a teenager, protesting against the Vietnam War and the death penalty, and campaigning for Aboriginal rights. After moving to London in 1971 he became involved with the Gay Liberation Front (GLF), organising demonstrations and helping devise the UK's first official Gay Pride march. Two years later, while in East Berlin for the World Festival of Youth and Students, Peter staged the first ever LGBTQ+ rights protest in a communist country, a move that ultimately led to him being detained and questioned by the secret police, the Stasi. In 1983, Peter ran as the Labour candidate in the Bermondsey by-election. His pro-LGBTQ+ and left-wing politics opened him up to horrifying abuse, death threats and homophobia. Ultimately, after alleged dirty tactics from his fellow candidates and a vicious tabloid press campaign against him, he lost the election. Nevertheless, by 1988 Peter was busy advocating for those living with HIV and struggling with AIDS-related illnesses. He set up the UK AIDS Vigil Organisation to defend the human rights of those affected by the disease, and was a founding member of the UK arm of HIV activist group ACT UP the following year.

In 1990, with the LGBTQ+ community facing increased discrimination and police victimisation due to the introduction of Section 28, Peter, together with other activists, created the queer rights direct-action group, OutRage! Within three years, they had successfully brought down arrest rates of gay and bisexual men by two-thirds. OutRage! also targeted church homophobia, interrupting the Easter Sermon of then-Archbishop of Canterbury, Dr George Carey, due to his support of anti-LGBTQ+ laws. This led to Peter's arrest.

He has been involved in challenging the victimisation of LGBTQ+ people in Russia, even venturing to the country in 2018. His one-man protest in front of the Kremlin highlighted the torture and murder of LGBT+ people in Chechnya and President Putin's collusion. He was once again arrested. In 2011, he was appointed director of the Peter Tatchell Foundation, a not-for-profit that seeks to promote and protect the human rights of individuals, communities and nations in the UK and around the world. He continues to fight for global LGBTQ+ equality and other human rights.

CHARITIES

CENTRAL

MERMAIDS

Office 3, 63 Charterhouse Street, EC1M 6HJ
mermaidsuk.org.uk
Nearest Tube: Barbican

Since 1995, Mermaids has been providing support for trans and gender-diverse children, young people and their families. Founded by parents of young trans people who wanted to keep their children safe, the charity is now one of the UK's leading LGBTQ+ organisations. Helping trans and gender-variant people under the age of 20, they have a help line that people can ring, as well as an online chat and text service and a digital forum. Mermaids also hosts residential weekends and local support groups for young people. Parents, guardians and family can also get in touch through the hotline, and there are specific digital parents' communities that can be accessed, too. Through their work, Mermaids reduces isolation and loneliness for trans and gender-variant young people, giving them and their loved ones the tools to navigate education and health services. With trans people under constant attack by the media and the public, Mermaids is an essential service – now, more than ever.

OPENING DOORS LONDON

Tavis House, 1-6 Tavistock Square, WC1H 9NA
openingdoorslondon.org.uk
Nearest Tube: Russell Square

Opening Doors London provides LGBTQ+ people over the age of 50 with support, advice, information and services. Hosting a number of events, visits to museums and galleries, film clubs, outings, coffee mornings and more, they also provide a befriending service for LGBTQ+ people over 50 who may feel isolated or lonely. Their services match people with a volunteer Befriender, who is on hand to provide social contact and company. This can include anything from accompanying someone to social groups and exhibitions, to just popping over for a cuppa. To complement these activities, they recently launched a telefriending service, which guarantees those who sign up a phone call from the same volunteer each week. As with many charities, Opening Doors offers training courses for care homes, hospitals, housing associations and more, to help others understand the needs of LGBTQ+ people over 50. Membership is required to take advantage of their services, but it's free to get involved. They accept inexperienced volunteers.

THE OUTSIDE PROJECT

Clerkenwell Fire Station, 40 Rosebery Ave,
Farringdon, EC1R 4RX
lgbtiqoutside.org

Launched by a group of LGBTQ+ people who worked in the homeless sector and had lived experience of homelessness, the Outside Project was created to fill a gap in provisions for marginalised groups. They provide sanctuary for queer people experiencing homelessness, who may otherwise have resisted access services because of a fear of anti-LGBTQ+ sentiments. Despite only launching to the public at London Pride in 2017, by the end of that summer the Outside Project had crowdfunded enough money to buy a 12-person tour bus. This became Britain's first homeless shelter for LGBTQ+ people. In 2019, after receiving funding from the Mayor's office, the Outside Project opened a permanent shelter and community centre in partnership with Stonewall Housing, based in an old Clerkenwell fire station. This crisis night shelter has space for 10 people across two shared and two private rooms, while the community centre provides help for those at risk of rough sleeping. It offers a hybrid of cultural and artistic programmes, social events, safe daytime refuge, a café and a LGBTQ+ library. Stonewall Housing provides housing advice and employment support, and the space is also utilised by a number of queer groups and businesses, including Lesbians and Gays Support the Migrants and the London offshoot of African Rainbow Family. In 2020, the Outside Project opened Star Refuge, a domestic abuse refuge for LGBTQ+ people in London. Not only does the Outside Project provide a safe and inclusive space for vulnerable queer people – they bring the entire community together.

STONEWALL
192 St John St, Clerkenwell, EC1V 4JY
stonewall.org.uk
Nearest Tube: Barbican

As the UK's largest LGBTQ+ charity, Stonewall provides a myriad of services. Their information line helps queer people find support and services by directing them to their own resources, as well as other organisations and charities. Stonewall also work with employers to help develop LGBTQ+ inclusive and diverse working environments, as well as training, consultancy and resources for teachers, schools and educational institutes to tackle bullying and bring LGBTQ+ identities into the curriculum. Alongside that, Stonewall conduct research and publish studies about issues affecting LGBTQ+ people, while lobbying and campaigning to ensure that the rights of the LGBTQ+ community are upheld.

CHARLIE CRAGGS

Born and raised in Ladbroke Grove, Charlie Craggs describes herself as a sensitive, typical Pisces. She was an introverted child – perhaps at odds with the self-professed sassy, gobby woman she is today. After finishing school, she enrolled at Central Saint Martins, where she did a foundation degree before moving on to study Creative Direction for Fashion at the London College of Fashion. During this period, after struggling with her mental health and experiencing suicidal ideation, Charlie decided to transition, aged 20.

It was in her final year at university in 2013 that she had the idea for Nail Transphobia. Initially conceived as part of her final coursework project, this was Charlie's attempt to show how activism could be fabulous. The concept was simple: as most people in the UK hadn't ever met a trans person, Charlie and a team of trans nail technicians travelled around with a pop-up salon, offering the public free manicures and the opportunity to talk. Their aim was to break misconceptions and make allies. Charlie, who had experienced bullying at school and further abuse when she transitioned, was aware of how important these conversations were in transforming public attitudes. As she says, she wanted to channel her trauma into something constructive. Nail Transphobia debuted at the V&A as part of the institution's LGBTQ+ history month programming. In the seven years since, Charlie has taken the project to festivals and universities up and down the UK. She was even invited to give a keynote speech at a big gala dinner at Cambridge University.

Charlie published her first book, *To My Trans Sisters*, in 2017. Featuring around 100 letters from trailblazing trans women from all different fields, the book was her attempt to provide solidarity, support and advice for other trans women, as many have no contacts in the trans community before they transition. That year, she made the *Independent's* Rainbow list, coming 40th in their list of the 101 most influential LGBTQ+ people in the UK. Charlie was also involved in the successful campaign to introduce a trans emoji, and regularly does public speaking and consultation with brands. In 2020, she began filming a documentary with the BBC about how trans people were being failed by the healthcare system and government. She also continues to work on Nail Transphobia.

HISTORY OF STONEWALL

Stonewall was formed to oppose Section 28, controversial and archaic legislation that banned the promotion or discussion of homosexuality in schools and by local authorities. The aims for the group were hashed out in September 1988, around the dining table at Sir Ian McKellen's house in Limehouse. The group of founding members and trustees (Sir Ian McKellen, Peter Ashman, Deborah Ballard, Duncan Campbell, Olivette Cole-Wilson, Lord Michael Cashman, Pam St Clement, Simon Fanshawe, Dorian Jabri, Matthew Parris, Lisa Power, Fiona Cunningham Reid, Dr Peter Rivas and Jennie Wilson) formally announced themselves on 24 May 1989. While Section 28 eventually became law, the organisation successfully campaigned and lobbied to equalise the age of consent, lift the ban on LGB people serving in the military, allow same-sex couples to adopt – and ultimately overthrow Section 28 entirely. They also helped usher in civil partnerships and same-sex marriage. In 2015, under the leadership of Baroness Ruth Hunt (since succeeded by Nancy Kelley) Stonewall became officially trans-inclusive. They advocate for the equality and rights of trans and gender non-conforming individuals, most recently around the proposed reform of the Gender Recognition Act. Currently, Stonewall are working hard to become fully inclusive of people on the asexual and aromantic spectrums, too. Those after a more comprehensive history of the charity should dig into Lord Michael Cashman's autobiography, *One of Them* (Bloomsbury, 2020).

NORTH

AKT

17-20 Parr St, N1 7GW
akt.org.uk
Nearest Tube: Old Street

Previously known as the Albert Kennedy Trust – named after 16-year-old Albert Kennedy, a vulnerable gay teenager who died after falling from the top of a Manchester multi-storey car park in 1989, having faced homophobic abuse – akt was the first ever service set up to help LGBTQ+ young people experiencing or facing homelessness. They provide safe homes, support and mentoring. Launched initially in Manchester by Cath Hall, an experienced foster carer who knew Kennedy, the organisation opened their London office in 1995. Given that 24% of all homeless young people identify as LGBTQ+, the work that akt does is essential. For over thirty years they have helped young queer people aged 16-25 to find emergency accommodation, access specialist support, develop skills and stay safe during crisis. In 2012, they opened Purple Door, the UK's first emergency safe house for LGBTQ+ youth. Today they have service centres in the north west, north east, Bristol and London. They help thousands of young LGBTQ+ people each year.

GALOP

356 Holloway Rd, N7 6PA
galop.org.uk
Nearest Tube: Holloway Road

GALOP is the UK's only specialist LGBTQ+ anti-violence charity. They provide advice, support and advocacy for anyone experiencing homophobia, transphobia, biphobia, sexual violence or domestic abuse, and help people report incidents to the right authorities. They run the National LGBT+ Domestic Abuse Hotline, which provides emotional and practical support and advice for queer folk who are experiencing domestic abuse and violence. They also launched the National LGBT+ Domestic Abuse Project, which aims to improve the infrastructure and support for reporting LGBTQ+ domestic abuse. GALOP conduct research and publish reports, including the Online Hate Crime Report.

GENDERED INTELLIGENCE

200A Pentonville Rd, N1 9JP
genderedintelligence.co.uk
Nearest Tube: King's Cross St. Pancras

Gendered Intelligence is a charity that supports trans and gender-variant individuals. Founded in 2008, they now operate across the UK. They specialise in support for young trans and gender-variant people aged 6-25, although their work to improve the quality of life for trans people covers all ages. Along with raising awareness, they operate regular activities for young trans people, community groups, residential trips, arts-based programming and mentoring. They also offer educational sessions and workshops; events for parents, carers and family members; and operate a network of therapists and counsellors.

LONDON FRIEND

86 Caledonian Rd, Islington, N1 9DN
londonfriend.org.uk
Nearest Tube: King's Cross St. Pancras

London Friend is the UK's oldest LGBTQ+ charity. Founded in 1972 as a befriending service from the Campaign for Homosexual Equality (CHE), it was originally comprised of a telephone helpline and social support groups, who met with those who felt isolated or who were coming out. In 1975, London Friend separated from CHE. Using a grant from the Home Office and Islington Council, they moved from their base in Earl's Court to Upper Street. They landed at their current location on Caledonian Road in 1987, and have offered a number of vital services ever since. Today, London Friend aids LGBTQ+ people in and around London, providing counselling and support for a number of issues, including relationships, gender identity, self-confidence and personal growth. Along with individual services, they organise groups run by trained volunteers. These vary from discussion and support groups to more socially focused meet-ups. They also run classes for those wanting to improve their spoken English and Pink Ink, a creative writing group. In 2011, London Friend merged with Antidote, the UK's oldest LGBTQ+ drug and alcohol service. They offer drop-in services, as well as specific advice and support for those involved in chemsex.

MOSAIC LGBT+ YOUNG PERSONS' TRUST

29-31 Hampstead Rd, NW1 3JA
mosaictrust.org.uk
Nearest Tube: Warren Street

Beginning its life as part of Brent Council's Youth Service in 2001, Mosaic is now one of the UK's leading LGBTQ+ youth charities. Previously known as Mosaic LGBT Youth Centre, the charity rebranded as Mosaic LGBT+ Young Persons' Trust in 2020 following the diversification of their offerings due to the COVID-19 crisis. They run a twice-weekly youth club for LGBTQ+ people under 19, as well as a cultural club, which gives access to theatre, art, literature and more. Face-to-face mentoring is available, and they encourage young LGBTQ+ people to volunteer with older folks from the community. Previous activities have included the Drag Academy, teaching young queer people about performing arts through drag, and the Flawless Talent Competition, which gave young LGBTQ+ artists the opportunity to perform on the main stage at Pride in London. In the last few years, they have offered a number of retreats and residential programmes, including a summer camp, which usually includes outdoor activities, workshops and group sessions. Mosaic also hosts annual events, such as the Pride Prom and Homoween, as an alternative to heteronormative school discos.

NATIONAL AIDS TRUST

Aztec House, 397-405 Archway Road, N6 4EY
nat.org.uk
Nearest Tube: Highgate

Formed in 1987, the National AIDS Trust's mission is to advocate and promote the health and wellbeing, dignity and rights of people living with or affected by HIV, and those who are at risk of HIV infection. Through guides, advice, education and advocacy they aim to increase awareness and understanding of HIV/AIDS and eradicate associated discrimination and inequality. In recent years their work has including campaigning for free HIV treatment for all patients living in England, preventing government cuts to national HIV prevention and advocating for the universal availability of PrEP. They even successfully took NHS England to court over their failure to consider providing the drug.

OUTCOME

35 Ashley Road, N19 3AG
islingtonmind.org.uk/our-services/outcome
Nearest Tube: Crouch Hill Overground Station

Outcome is Islington Mind's LGBTQ+ off shoot. They provide queer people with a safe space to receive therapy, learn new skills and acquire knowledge. Their specialist services and activities include Free From Fear To Love, which helps newly 'out' LGBTQ+ asylum seekers and refugees; United in Strength, which supports lesbian, bisexual, queer and trans women who experience domestic violence; and RainbowSports@Mind, which aims to reduce isolation through sports and movement. They also have a singing group, a creative writing group, a walking group and more.

POSITIVELY UK

St Mark's Studios, 14 Chillingworth Rd, N7 8QJ
positivelyuk.org
Nearest Tube: Holloway Road

Since 1987, Positively UK has provided peer-led support for people living with HIV. They help people with every aspect of their diagnosis, their health care and their life with HIV. Started initially as a group for women living with HIV, the organisation soon found that the wider community needed to engage more with each other, in order to find adequate emotional and practical support. Today, they offer a wide range of services, including peer mentoring, support

groups for those under 30 and over 50, a women's space and their Recently Diagnosed Workshop. This interactive workshop, taking place over two days, welcomes people who have been living with HIV for under three years.

STONEWALL HOUSING

Leroy House, 436 Essex Rd, N1 3QP
stonewallhousing.org
Nearest Tube: Angel

Not to be confused with the other major LGBTQ+ charity, Stonewall Housing has been creating safe spaces for queer people since 1983. As an organisation, it provides LGBTQ+ people with free advice, information and casework services on homelessness, housing options, harassment and accommodation access. In addition to weekly and monthly drop ins, employability workshops and training services; Stonewall Housing offer consultancy for businesses and organisations on how they can better support their LGBTQ+ staff, customers and members. They implement various initiatives that focus on groups within the LGBTQ+ community, such as survivors of domestic abuse, older queer people and LGBTQ+ young people. In 2019, Stonewall Housing formed their ambassadors' program, the House of Stonewall. This diverse group of service users, alumni, donors and champions want to raise awareness and funding for Stonewall Housing, to ensure their vital services continue.

TERRENCE HIGGINS TRUST

Cally Yard, 437-439 Caledonian Road, N7 9BG
tht.org.uk
Nearest Tube: King's Cross St Pancras

Named after Terry Higgins, one of the first people to die of AIDS-related illnesses in the UK, the Terrence Higgins Trust (then the Terry Higgins Trust) was launched in 1982 by Terry's close friends Martyn Butler and Tony Calvert, and Terry's partner Rupert Whitaker. At the time, HIV and AIDS were known as 'Gay-Related Immune Deficiency', or GRID. Their goal was to raise both awareness and money, in order to fund research into HIV and AIDS. In 1983, with the help of Tony Whitehead, the organisation was formalised, gaining charitable status by 1984. Since then, the Terrence Higgins Trust has been one of the leading HIV/AIDS organisations in the UK, fighting for the rights and needs of those living with HIV. In more recent years, the organisation has diversified further, developing sexual health services both for those living with or at risk of HIV, and the broader population. This involves testing for HIV and sexually transmitted infections, support for those living with HIV, sexual health advice and information, free condoms, therapy and council sessions and more. Some of their work with more marginalised groups, such as older women and the trans community, is done in partnerships with other organisations, a tradition that runs through the charity's DNA. The Terrence Higgins Trust has also been involved in the campaign to make PrEP available on the NHS.

WISE THOUGHTS

2nd Floor, Wood Green Library, High Rd, N22 6XD
wisethoughts.org
Nearest Tube: Turnpike Lane

This local arts charity was formed in 1999. They work with LGBTQ+ and Black, Asian and Minority Ethnic artists, filmmakers, producers, creators and communities both in the UK and abroad. Through a number of arts programmes, events, exhibitions, dance recitals and performances, Wise Thoughts gives queer people of colour an opportunity to share and explore their experiences, identities and creative works. Previous initiatives include 'SHIVer', a multi-media performance project about South Asian women and HIV; 'Un-tender Touch', which explored domestic violence through dance; and 'Flames', a multi-media project that focused on the sexual health of young BAME people in Hertfordshire. More recently, Wise Thoughts have launched 'WiseOut!', a programme that tackles homophobia, biphobia and transphobia in schools by using arts and media to explore different sexualities and gender identities. They also host regular drop-in meet-ups for LGBTQ+ people aged 16 and over from their base in Haringey, as well as spots in Tottenham and Muswell Hill. These offer a safe space for queer people to gather and discuss art, watch live performances and get advice. Specific drop-ins for LGBTQ+ people aged between 11-19 are also on offer, as are workshops, yoga and dance classes. Each year, Wise Thoughts host London's GFEST, an LGBTQ+ arts festival that includes dance, music, drag, film screenings, art exhibitions, debates, readings, comedy and talks.

EAST

EAST LONDON OUT PROJECT (ELOP)
56-60 Grove Road, Walthamstow, E17 9BN
elop.org
Nearest Tube: Walthamstow Central

Since 1995, the East London Out Project (ELOP) has provided support for lesbian, gay, bisexual, transgender and queer folk living in east and north London. With a focus on mental health and physical wellbeing, they offer a wide range of services, including advice, advocacy, counselling, youth services, sexual health services, and social and community activities. They also operate a community hub and café, where members of the LGBTQ+ community can pop in for a cuppa, access information and meet new people.

IMAAN UK
159 Mile End Rd, Bethnal Green, E1 4AQ
imaan.org.uk
Nearest Tube: Stepney Green

Imaan is the UK's leading LGBTQ+ Muslim charity. Founded in 1999 in response to the white, cisgender gay male focus of the country's queer scene, Imaan's mission is to empower and support LGBTQ+ Muslims, who often find themselves affected by homophobia, transphobia and islamophobia. Led by and working for LGBTQ+ Muslims, Imaan campaign to create cohesion between people's culture, sexuality, gender, family and faith. In 2019, they set about fundraising to host the first ever Muslim Pride in London. ImaanFest was due to take place in April 2020, but was postponed due to the COVID-19 pandemic. 'We want to provide a safe and inclusive space where people feel like they do not have to choose between identities and that they can be LGBTQI and Muslim without pressure from those who say otherwise,' the charity told the *Independent*. 'Our festival will provide a space for LGBTQI Muslims from across the UK to be empowered, engaged and to make no apologies for being practising Muslims and LGBTQI People.'

KALEIDOSCOPE TRUST
The Print House Studio, 18 Ashwin Street, E8 3DL
kaleidoscopetrust.com
Nearest Tube: Dalston Kingsland/Dalston Junction Overground

The Kaleidoscope Trust believes that LGBTQ+ people all over the world should be free, safe and equal. Founded in 2011, this non-profit organisation works to ensure that the human rights of LGBTQ+ people around the world are enforced in countries where people can be persecuted, discriminated against and marginalised because of their sexuality, gender identity or expression, or both. They support local LGBTQ+ activists in over 50 countries; inform the British public about the UK's role in spreading discriminatory, anti-LGBTQ legislation during colonialism; and inspire individuals to create change. In 2019, Phyll Opoku-Gyimah (also known as Lady Phyll (see page 174)), the co-founder of UK Black Pride, was made Executive Director of the trust, making her the first Black woman to head up a mainstream LGBTQ+ organisation in the UK.

RUTH HUNT

Ruth Hunt may have been born in Wales, but as the Baroness of Bethnal Green she has more than earned her status as a Londoner. Born in 1980, she was studious growing up, reading English Literature and Language at Oxford University, where she was elected President of the Student Union. Moving to London in 2004, she joined the Equality Challenge Unit, which improves equality and diversity among staff and students in higher education. While here, she made the case that universities should be engaged and interested in inclusion issues, such as why LGBTQ+ students may not be able to get a student loan because of strained parental relations, or why Black students don't experience the same opportunities as other students.

In 2005, a week after the 7/7 bombings, she started at LGBTQ+ charity Stonewall as a senior policy officer. In that role, Ruth developed an evidence base for social change. This included organising research into LGBTQ+ hate crimes and commissioning the first study into lesbian health. Working her way up through various roles, including Head of Policy and Research and Director of Public Affairs, Ruth was named as the organisation's Chief Executive in 2014. Her vision for the charity centred on changing hearts and minds, transforming institutions, changing the law, and empowering individuals around the world. Under her leadership, the organisation's remit expanded to include the transgender community for the first time.

In 2019, after five years in the role, Ruth stepped down as Chief Executive of Stonewall. Later that year, she was nominated for a life peerage, and in October 2019 she was accepted into the House of Lords, becoming Baroness Ruth of Bethnal Green. Ruth currently runs a business, Deeds + Words, with her partner Caroline Ellis, and in 2020 she edited and published her first book, Queer Prophets, a collection of writings by prominent LGBTQ+ figures such as Amrou Al-Kadhi, Jeanette Winterson, Dustin Lance Black and Lady Phyll on what it means to be queer and religious.

POSITIVE EAST

159 Mile End Rd, Bethnal Green, E1 4AQ
positiveeast.org.uk
Nearest Tube: Stepney Green

For nearly 30 years, Positive East has been providing support and services for people living with, or affected by, HIV. Their mission is to 'improve the quality of life of individuals and communities affected by HIV', something they achieve through promoting safe sex and providing HIV tests, holistic services, counselling, support groups, peer support, workshops, classes and more. Each year for World AIDS Day, they host the Red Run, a charity fun run to raise money for HIV services, charities and organisations.

SOUTH

LGBT HERO

Unit 22, The Link Business Centre,
49 Effra Rd, SW2 1BZ
gmfa.org.uk
Nearest Tube: Brixton

LGBT HERO is the health equality and rights organisation for LGBTQ+ people. They formed in 1992 as a way to help LGBTQ+ folk make informed choices and decisions regarding their health and wellbeing, and to confront health inequalities affecting LGBTQ+ people. The organisation acts as the parent organisation for GMFA, the gay men's health project, and OutLife, an online hub and digital community where LGBTQ+ people can find information, advice and support about mental and sexual health. They also publish *FS* magazine, a gay and bisexual men's health magazine that also touches on the challenges of modern gay life.

UK LESBIAN & GAY IMMIGRATION GROUP

7-14 Great Dover St, SE1 4YR
uklgig.org.uk
Nearest Tube: Borough.

With the number of LGBTQ+ people applying for asylum in the UK rising, the UK Lesbian & Gay Immigration Group provides information and support for queer asylum seekers and those wishing to settle in the UK to be with partners. Along with providing advice and legal information, UKLGIG also gives LGBTQ+ asylum seekers emotional support to boost self-esteem and reduce isolation. Their work involves research, policy work, training and campaigning for the improved treatment of those seeking asylum.

NO FIXED ABODE

AFRICAN RAINBOW FAMILY
africanrainbowfamily.org

Established in 2014 in response to anti-gay laws and homophobia in some of the Commonwealth countries in Africa, the African Rainbow Family is a non-profit charity that helps lesbian, gay, bisexual, transgender, intersex and queer people of African heritage, as well as people from wider Black, Asian and minority ethnic groups. They provide advice and support for LGBTQ+ refugees and asylum seekers, organise social events, offer free counselling and even provide hot meals. Their goal is global LGBTQ+ equality, and they work to ensure the dignity and safety of LGBTQ+ people who have immigration issues related to their sexual or gender identity.

ALL ABOUT TRANS
allabouttrans.org.uk

All About Trans is a project from On Road. It aims to shift how the media portrays, discusses and understands trans people. Founded in 2011, it looks at all the ways that media professionals and organisations can improve their trans representation at a time when media depictions of trans people are often dehumanising, poor and offensive. They have worked with the BBC and Channel 4, running peer support meet-ups, media communication training and more.

LGBT HUMANISTS
facebook.com/LGBTHumanistsUK

Set up in response to the 1976 blasphemy case launched by Mary Whitehouse against LGBTQ+ newspaper *Gay News*, the LGBT Humanists have stood against religious homophobia and advocated for LGBTQ+ rights since 1979. Their platforms have included equalising the age of consent, the introduction of equal marriage and the banning of conversion therapy. For years, the organisation's president was writer and activist Maureen Duffy. It is now presided over by Stuart McCaighy, who holds the role of chair in a voluntary capacity. The LGBT Humanists support demonstrations, organise talks and public meetings, and even offer LGBTQ+ humanist wedding ceremonies.

QUEER BRITAIN
queerbritain.org.uk

Queer Britain is working towards being the UK's first LGBTQ+ museum. Since 2018, the charity has been campaigning and fundraising, with support from the London Mayor's Office and corporate sponsors. It hopes to soon find a space that will house permanent and temporary exhibitions, immersive experiences, and historical and cultural queer artefacts, as well as multifaceted spaces available to the wider LGBTQ+ community. 'People came out of their closets, now it's time to come out of the margins,' said the museum's CEO Joseph Galliano. 'Queer Britain will be the first national museum for all, regardless of sexuality and gender identity, to fully celebrate and reflect the lives of LGBTQ+ people of all backgrounds. It will help complete the nation's family tree.'

A mural from Vauxhall One, in partnership with Network Rail, celebrating the queer history of Vauxhall Pleasure Gardens.

E
FERENT
LOVE
UXHALL
auxhall
LONDON
BEINVAUXHALL
INVAUXHALL.COM

REGARD
regard.org.uk

Established in 1989, Regard is a national organisation of lesbians, gay men, bi, trans and queer people who self-identify as disabled. As a registered charity, they provide support, information and advice for any disabled LGBTQ+ person, while also raising awareness for disability issues within the queer community. They believe that society needs to remove the stigma and barriers that affect disabled people, in order to become truly inclusive. Regard also support disabled LGBTQ+ people who struggle with social isolation.

SWITCHBOARD
switchboard.lgbt

Switchboard began life in 1974 in an upstairs room at Housmans bookshop in King's Cross. Since then it has grown and grown, providing London's LGBTQ+ community with a safe space for support, advice and discussion. While it previously ran for 24 hours a day, the lines are now operated between 10am and 10pm, 365 days a year. They accept calls from all over the UK. The lines are managed by trained volunteers and calls are completely confidential. People call about everything, from relationship advice, how to deal with homophobic abuse, information about local gay venues and support for LGBTQ+ young people who may need a safe space to stay. You can also contact Switchboard via instant messaging from their website and via email. No matter what you want to talk about, Switchboard is there to listen.

TONIC
tonicliving.org.uk

Tonic is a charity working to create inclusive, urban LGBTQ+ retirement communities in the UK. Founded in 2014, they have learned from similar initiatives around the world. Together with housing and care providers, as well as other LGBTQ+ organisations, Tonic hope to develop new communities in London.

THE SWITCHBOARD STORY

Founded in 1974, the London Lesbian and Gay Switchboard is one of the oldest queer organisations in the UK. Initially operating for five hours each day from the basement in Housmans bookshop, King's Cross, the demand for Switchboard's services meant that just over a year later, these volunteer-run lines were operating around the clock. Requests could deal with anything from where the best party in town was that night, to relationship and family advice. Callers would even ring to be reminded about the hanky code. Switchboard also provided information about police raids, which were common occurrences at LGBTQ+ venues in the '70s and '80s. People rung to inform volunteers that raids had happened or were about to occur.

During the 1980s, Switchboard, already a life line for so many, took on an additional role, providing information about HIV/AIDS during a period when mainstream media, health services and politicians knew little about it. The government even included the number on their 'Don't Die of Ignorance' pamphlets, which were distributed to every household in 1987. Switchboard moved out from Housmans in 1993. During this decade, many of the calls focused on the implementation of the draconian Section 28, a policy banning the 'promotion of homosexuality in schools and by local authorities', as well as safe sex advice. In 1999, following the bombing at the Admiral Duncan, Switchboard were on hand for London's queer community. They were even consulted by the police, following the damning results of the Stephen Lawrence review, which revealed their lack of support for the LGBTQ+ community in London at that time.

The Lesbian and Gay Switchboard still provides its services to this day. They changed their name in 2015 to just 'Switchboard', so as not to exclude anyone from across the LGBTQ+ spectrum. People still call with issues about loneliness or relationships, for help coming out, sexual health advice and information about where they can meet other LGBTQ+ people in their area. Switchboard also receive calls from teachers, parents, guardians and social workers. In 2019, they launched their critically acclaimed podcast, *The Log Books*, which looks back through the documentation of every caller and the topic of their call. Featuring memories, entries from the log books and interviews with queer folk, callers and volunteers, it won the Best New Podcast at the British Podcast Awards in 2020.

WORLD AIDS DAY RED RUN

The World AIDS Day Red Run is a 5km/10km charity fun run (or a 5km walk if you prefer), organised by Positive East. Running – literally – since 2009, it has raised over £500,000 for HIV services and organisations across the UK. For the last few years, the run has taken place at Victoria Park in East London. In 2019 it was introduced by Sir Ian McKellen and the fabulous drag queen pop group Denim. Social media stars the Cock Destroyers were seen running to raise money for the Terrence Higgins Trust.

THE ARTS

CENTRAL

PERFORMING ARTS

SOHO THEATRE
21 Dean St, Soho, W1D 3NE
sohotheatre.com
Nearest Tube: Tottenham Court Road

The Soho Theatre spent the '70s and '80s in the basement of a former building owned by the University of Westminster (then the Polytechnic of Central London). In the '90s, the theatre had a more nomadic existence, travelling to venues around London such as the ICA and the Royal Court, before spending a prolonged period at the Cockpit Theatre in Marylebone. In 2000, however, it returned to Soho in a new, purpose-built theatre on Dean Street, where it sits today.

Soho Theatre hosts some of the best up-and-coming talent from around the world, nurturing developing writers and artists. Be it comedy, musical, theatre, cabaret, drag or spoken word, you'll find it all here. The theatre operates schemes to bring in new work, and offers mentorships and development programmes for emerging artists. An emphasis is put on work by LGBTQ+ creators. The venue sports a bustling bar, always packed with people seeing shows at one of their three theatres, as well as those out on the town for drinks.

The Soho Theatre highlights work by LGBTQ+ creators.

NORTH

PERFORMING ARTS

KING'S HEAD THEATRE
115 Upper St, The Angel, N1 1QN
kingsheadtheatre.com
Nearest Tube: Highbury and Islington/Angel

Founded in 1970 as the first pub theatre in London since the days of Shakespeare, the King's Head Theatre has a reputation for housing some of the best fringe theatre in London, including LGBTQ+ works. Joanna Lumley and Hugh Grant have graced the stage, and in 2015 it hosted the premiere of *Shock Treatment*, the sequel to *The Rocky Horror Show*. Their productions often transfer to the West End, including their 2019 production of Kevin Elyot's seminal gay play, *Coming Clean*, and they successfully fundraised for the theatre to move to Islington Square in 2020. Definitely check out their Christmas panto – it's always a sell-out.

LONDON GAY MEN'S CHORUS
The Old Town Hall, 213 Haverstock Hill, NW3 4QP
lgmc.org.uk
Nearest Tube: Belsize Park

The London Gay Men's Chorus began its life in 1991. Founded by nine gay men who used to meet at London Friend, then a social group and befriending service, their first 'gig' was a charity show outside Angel Station to raise money for the Terrence Higgins Trust. Singing covers of songs like 'Somewhere Over the Rainbow', the show proved so popular that they had to shut the station. Since then, the LGMC has become the biggest gay choir in Europe, boasting over 200 members and performing sold out shows across London and the world. They have worked with artists like Mark Ronson and Elton John, and appeared on TV shows, including *Top of the Pops*.

The LGMC is remembered for performing at the memorial following the Admiral Duncan bombing in 1999 (see page 14), and for their moving rendition of Simon & Garfunkel's 'Bridge Over Troubled Water', which they performed during the Soho vigil following the shooting at Pulse in Orlando, Florida. Other notable covers include their version of Tom Robinson Band's '(Sing If You're) Glad To Be Gay', which gets performed at almost every LGMC concert, as well as versions of Lady Gaga's 'Born This Way' and Lily Allen's 'Fuck You'. If you're keen on joining, new members are welcome, although there is a lengthy waiting list and the rehearsal schedule is rigid. Wannabe Whitney's should also know that within the choir is an elite contingent known as the Ensemble: a group of auditioned singers who are the 'rapid-response' unit of the choir. They perform at high-profile events across Europe and during times when the full choir is too large to perform.

OLLY ALEXANDER

As the frontman of Years & Years, Olly Alexander has produced some of UK's finest pop music through an unashamedly and explicitly queer lens, picking up Number 1 hits, best-selling albums and legions of fans on the way. Born in 1990 and growing up between Blackpool and the Forest of Dean, he moved to London when he was 18 to pursue acting, starring in films like Gaspar Noé's *Enter the Void*, Roger Michell's *Le Week-end* and Lone Scherfig's *The Riot Club*, as well as TV shows such as *Skins* and *Penny Dreadful*. By 2010, he had met bandmates Mikey Goldsworthy and Emre Türkmen. They began writing music and playing shows around London at spots like Proud Galleries and The Lexington. The band signed a two-single deal with electronic label Kitsune in 2014, which later mutated into a record deal with a major label, Polydor. Following a string of singles, including Number 1 hit 'King', the band's first album, *Communion*, was released in 2015. It debuted at Number 1 on the UK Chart, and went on to sell over 1 million copies. Olly's songwriting was notable not only for his tight and infectious melodies but for his lyrics, which touched on his experiences with depression and anxiety, and which often utilised same-sex pronouns. This intensified on the group's second album, 2019's *Palo Santo*, which saw Olly assert his queerness through homoerotic and religious imagery, with songs that sanctified gay sex and dove into the murky waters of desire.

In 2017, he produced a documentary for the BBC, *Olly Alexander: Growing Up Gay*. This documentary explored why LGBTQ+ people disproportionally experience mental health issues and saw Olly open up about his own experiences with depression, coming out and disordered eating. It cemented what is at the heart of everything he does: advocating for and lifting up the LGBTQ+ community. Through sharing his own experiences and living openly, Olly has helped break down stigmas surrounding mental health and LGBTQ+ issues. He also uses his platform to speak about safe sex, equality, HIV testing and access to PrEP. His latest projects include a role in Russell T Davies's drama *It's A Sin*, which explores the lives of gay men and the impact of the AIDS crisis, as well as Years & Years' third album.

EAST

PERFORMING ARTS

ARCOLA QUEER COLLECTIVE
24 Ashwin St, Dalston, E8 3DL
arcolatheatre.com
Nearest Tube: Dalston Junction Overground

The Arcola Theatre in Dalston produces some of the most groundbreaking, diverse and bold performing and visual arts in London. With an emphasis on inclusion, accessibility and quality, they champion new and emerging artists, performers and creatives to make their visions a reality. Part of this entails engaging with the local community, which includes youth projects, courses and community groups. One such group is the Arcola Queer Collective, a performance squad of LGBTQ+ people formed in 2014 who explore queer identity and its theatrical presentation. Open to all LGBTQ+ folk and with annual calls for new members, they host a number of performances each year, with previous members including cabaret stars Rubyyy Jones, Travis Alabanza, Miss Cairo and Sam Reynolds, as well as actors Dan de la Motte, Damien Hughes, Temi Wilkey and Lotte Vallis. Any member can suggest an idea or performance for consideration, and in the past the collective has hosted a queer arts festival, takes on *A Midsummer Night's Dream* and Antoine de Saint-Exupéry's *The Little Prince*, and new work by up-and-coming writers. In 2018, they published *Global Queer Plays: Seven LGBTQ Works From Around the World*, a collection of short plays that explored how queer stories are depicted and told worldwide.

FESTIVALS

FAGGAMUFFIN BLOC PARTY
facebook.com/FaggamuffinBlocParty
Nearest Tube: Hackney Central Overground

With a mission to increase the visibility of QTIPOC Pride at carnivals, the Faggamuffin Bloc Party has been running since 2018. This is a soundsystem run by and for queer people of colour. Working collaboratively with Hackney Pride 365, they host an all-day party on the Sunday of Hackney Carnival. In 2019, they secured funding from Arts Council England, taking this party to another level with a headline performance from Lady Leshurr. In 2020, they also secured funding from ACE to create an online space for queer, trans and intersex people of colour amidst the COVID-19 pandemic. In the words of Faggamuffin Bloc Party's project director, Virginia Wilson: 'Caribbean Carnival is more than an everyday festival and Faggamuffin Bloc Party more than just another sound system; it is a reclaiming of a tradition of resistance and liberation through celebration by and for queer people of colour.'

SOUTH

PERFORMING ARTS

ABOVE THE STAG THEATRE
72 Albert Embankment, Vauxhall, SE1 7TP
abovethestag.org.uk
Nearest Tube: Vauxhall

In 2008, an Australian thespian living in London had the idea to create a theatre that specifically showcased gay-related works. Finding a space above the Stag pub in Victoria, the aptly named Above the Stag Theatre was born. During the redevelopment of Victoria, the pub was bulldozed and in 2013 the theatre was moved to Vauxhall, keeping the name despite the butchered Stag. The theatre relocated to its current spot under the Vauxhall arches again in 2018 and now, as the UK's only dedicated LGBTQ+ theatre, it showcases a variety of plays, musicals, cabaret, readings, comedy and every kind of entertainment that you can imagine. Complete with two performance spaces and a bar, the theatre puts on new work from up-and-coming writers, as well as revivals and classics. They also host exhibitions and other events.

FESTIVALS

BFI FLARE: LONDON LGBTIQ+ FILM FESTIVAL
BFI, Belvedere Rd, Bishop's, SE1 8XT
bfi.org.uk/flare
Nearest Tube: Waterloo

The BFI has run some kind of gay and lesbian film programme since 1986, although the first official 'London Lesbian and Gay Film Festival' was in 1988. The name was changed in 2014 to BFI Flare, to better represent the spectrum of queer cinema that the film festival showcased. Taking place in March each year and usually separated into themes – Hearts, Bodies, Minds and special presentations – the festival is home to feature films, documentaries, shorts and classic cinema. Alongside the film screenings, the Flare festival hosts a number of panels, talks, Q&As and events, including the closing night club night, which is always rammed with queers who know how to party. There is usually some digital programming to complement things too, and as always you can check out the BFI's LGBT Britain archive, some of which is also accessible online. The BFI run LGBTQ+ programming under the Flare banner throughout the rest of the year.

MIGHTY HOOPLA FESTIVAL
mightyhoopla.com

Established by the superfabulous talent team behind Sink the Pink (see page 30), the Mighty Hoopla is a day-festival with a focus on pop music and queer culture. Featuring drag performers, lip syncing, voguing, dancing and pop ups from the likes of Hungama and The Glory, along with some of the biggest, best and most nostalgic names in music, this a true pop extravaganza. Previous headliners include Years & Years, TLC and Chaka Khan, while acts like All Saints, Lily Allen, MNEK, Liberty X, Will Young and Mel C have all performed. In 2019, the festival moved from its previous home in East London to Brockwell Park.

NO FIXED ABODE

THE BITTEN PEACH
instagram.com/bittenpeachuk

The Bitten Peach is a pan-Asian performance and arts collective made up of some of London's most fabulous drag stars, burlesque icons, musicians and cabaret legends, including ShayShay, Jason Kwan, Evelyn Carnate, Marianne Cheesecake, Mahatma Khandi, Sigi Moonlight, Aurora Starr and Lilly SnatchDragon. Taking its name from an ancient tale of Zhou Dynasty China, the phrase 'bitten peach' is a euphemism for homosexuality. This collective has operated since 2019.

THE COCOA BUTTER CLUB
thecocoabutterclub.com

The Cocoa Butter Club exists as a 'creative clapback'. Faced with a queer arts and cabaret scene that is overwhelmingly white and riddled with cultural appropriation, this Black-facing cabaret collective was born to centre, showcase and celebrate performers of colour. Comprised of QTIPOC (queer, trans and intersex people of colour) performers, musicians, dancers and drag artistes, you can find everything from voguing to burlesque, tied together by R&B, Neo-soul, blues and jazz at the Cocoa Butter Club. They have appeared at Southbank Centre, Dalston Superstore, the RVT and the Roundhouse.

THE GAY MEN'S DANCE COMPANY
thegmdc.com

Founded in 2015, the Gay Men's Dance Company offers dance classes, drama classes and even choir lessons. They also run a male-only pole dancing class, as well as yoga and martial arts. Alongside that, the GMDC has a thriving social community, organising various trips, parties and get togethers for its members. They regularly perform at Pride in London and host an annual charity variety show at the Troxy, East London.

LESLEY MAGAZINE
lesleymagazine.co.uk

Lesley Magazine is a free zine, arts collective and digital space created by and for queer womxn, trans and non-binary people and allies. Under the guidance of Kat Hudson and with a small editorial team, the zine and bustling Instagram account share news, listings, nightlife recommendations and art. With an accessible DIY approach, Lesley makes space for unheard queer voices, nurtures their talent and expression, and provides a platform for them to thrive.

THE PINK SINGERS
pinksingers.co.uk

Formed in 1983, the Pink Singers claim the title of Europe's longest running LGBTQ+ choir. Formed 7 April 1983, they have played shows all over the world, teaming up with numerous LGBTQ+ organisations. They even provided backing vocals for '80s pop group Bronski Beat on their debut album *Age of Consent* in 1984. The first women joined the group in 1988, and since then the choir has welcomed all LGBTQ+ people into its ranks – though any budding choristers must audition. Each year they perform two main concerts in London, along with a smattering of smaller performances with LGBTQ+ choirs from across the globe.

QUEER ART AND MUSEUMS IN LONDON

It's impossible to signpost all the queer art in London. It sprouts from galleries across the city, from recreations of Michelangelo's David at the V&A to Keith Haring's work at Rhodes Contemporary Art. There is, of course, Tate Modern, which hosted a large Gilbert & George retrospective in 2007; and the Tate Britain, whose large-scale exhibition of LGBTQ+ British art, 'Queer British Art: 1861–1967', took over the space in 2017.

While the queerness of art and artists is often unknowable, some institutions are attempting to demystify things: the V&A offer free queer tours of the museum, headed up by the spritely Dan Vo and a coterie of volunteers. Similarly, the British Museum has its 'Desire, love, identity: LGBTQ histories trail', while the National Portrait Gallery offers the occasional LGBTQ+ tour.

If you're looking for smaller galleries who focus on representing queer and gender non-conforming artists, check out Arcadia Missa and Project Native Informant. It's also worth keeping abreast of what LGBTQ+ programming galleries and museums might be planning during Pride.

QUEER THEATRE IN THE WEST END

Along with the Soho Theatre, which regularly produces LGBTQ+ plays, cabaret, comedy and performances, the main West End theatres have a history of queer productions. Along with musicals like *Hairspray* and *La Cage aux Folles*, which often pop up for a run, and newcomers like *Everybody's Talking About Jamie* at the Apollo Theatre and *&Juliet* at the Shaftesbury, the West End has housed *The Boys in the Band*, David Mamet's *Boston Marriage* and *My Night with Reg*. In 1979, a transfer of gay play *Bent*, which starred Sir Ian McKellen, moved from the Royal Court Theatre in Sloane Square to the West End. Most recently, in 2018, Matthew Lopez's two-part epic, *The Inheritance* (based loosely on E. M. Forster's *Howard's End* and starring Vanessa Redgrave), transferred from its run at the Young Vic to the Noel Coward Theatre, where it ran until the beginning of 2019. The West End also sees regular productions of plays by queer writers, including Tennessee Williams and Alan Bennett.

DR JU GOSLING (AKA JU90)

Born in 1962 and raised in Essex, Ju Gosling realised by the age of 16 that she didn't have the body for ballet due to spinal curvature. Still, her interest in art, writing and theatre prevailed, and after setting up a fanzine in Norwich following her first degree in film and English studies, she pivoted to journalism. Moving to London in the mid-1980s, Gosling was hired to start a tenants' newspaper, funded by the now defunct Greater London Council. It was during this time that, as a member of the National Union of Journalists (NUJ), Gosling made a complaint against a fellow journalist's conduct after they published a piece outing a woman who had worked at a Lambeth homelessness service as trans. After successfully preventing further transphobic reporting, Gosling ended up chairing the NUJ's equality council, where she worked to reposition the reporting on HIV/AIDS in the UK.

In the 1990s, Gosling began experiencing chronic spinal pain due to an undiagnosed fracture resulting from an underlying genetic condition. In 1997, while living in Cornwall, she was prescribed a spinal brace. On what today would be considered a blog, she explored the social constructions of disability and transformed her experiences into performance art and self-portraits. That same year, she became the first person in the UK to present her PhD, which was about girls' school stories, as a website. Returning to journalism, Gosling experienced barriers, specifically at a conference that the NUJ held on the West coast of Ireland in 2000. After finding the venue inaccessible, Gosling suffered from illness and had to be flown home. It was an illness she never fully recovered from. She did, however, successfully take the NUJ to a tribunal, where they were found guilty on four counts of discrimination, two of them major; and of personal injury.

Since then, Gosling has focused on her art, which has seen her collaborate with the Tate Modern and the Science Museum, and exhibit all over the UK, both in solo and group shows. She is currently the artistic director of Together! 2012 CIC, an Arts Council England National Portfolio Organisation that hosts year-round programming focused on Disability Arts and Human Rights, as well as an annual festival. Gosling also co-chairs Regard, the national LGBTQ+ organisation for people who self-identify as disabled. Regard work voluntarily year-round, advocating for the rights of disabled LGBTQI+ people, particularly in terms of improving social care and reducing hate crime. Artistically, her current focus is on poetry and spoken word.

QUEER ARCHIVES

BISHOPSGATE INSTITUTE
230 Bishopsgate, Spitalfields, EC2M 4QH
bishopsgate.org.uk
Nearest Tube: Liverpool Street

Established as a library and centre for culture and learning in 1895, the Bishopsgate Institute houses a cavernous LGBTQ+ archive. Housed in their Special Collections and Archives, this selection covers the late 19th century onwards, containing archives from Stonewall, Switchboard, the Terrence Higgins Trust and way more. Bishopsgate is also home to the Lesbian and Gay Newsmedia Archive (LAGNA), which contains 300,000 press cuttings from the heterosexual press, and a vast amount of LGBTQ+ publications, literature, journals, biographies and pamphlets. You'll find masses of ephemera too, including pins, banners and outfits, as well as personal materials, photographs, diaries and quite literally anything else you can think of. The Special Collections and Archives also hosts the UK Leather and Fetish Archives, if you're interested in exploring the history of fetish, kink and BDSM in the UK.

Unlike a lot of other archives, you don't need to make an appointment to get stuck in. Just register with the staff and pack away your bag in a locker (no pens, water or snacks allowed, naturally). Talking of the staff, they are incredibly helpful and welcoming. Special Collections and Archives Manager, Stef Dickers, is a fountain of knowledge and will know how to help you, even if you're not sure where to start. He runs tours of the archives, which give you an informative and entertaining insight into their system. Alongside these tours, Bishopsgate hosts talks, panels and LGBTQ+ history fairs, as well as cultural and educational programmes. If you have any interest in LGBTQ+ history or culture, the Bishopsgate Institute is an essential resource: truly a hidden gem in the world of queer London.

THE HALL-CARPENTER ARCHIVES AT LSE LIBRARY: THE BRITISH LIBRARY OF POLITICAL AND ECONOMIC SCIENCE
10 Portugal St, Holborn, WC2A 2HD
lse.ac.uk/library/collection-highlights/lgbt-collections
Nearest Tube: Holborn

Founded in 1982, the Hall-Carpenter Archives is one of the biggest collections of historical records, ephemera and printed materials that document LGBTQ+ activism in the UK since the 1950s. Born out of the work of the Campaign for Homosexual Equality (CHE) and named after the writers Radclyffe Hall and Edward Carpenter, in 1988 the archive found a home at the London School of Economics Library. The collection is open to the public, although visitors need to book to visit and request materials before they arrive. The Hall-Carpenter Archives press cuttings collection, the Lesbian and Gay Newsmedia Archive (LAGNA), can be found at the Bishopsgate Institute, while the Hall-Carpenter Archives Oral History Project, which contains interviews with lesbians and gay men, can be found at the British Library National Sound Archive.

LESBIAN GAY BISEXUAL TRANSGENDER COMMUNITY ARCHIVES AT THE LONDON METROPOLITAN ARCHIVES

The Finsbury Business Centre, 40 Northampton Rd, Farringdon, EC1R 0HB

cityoflondon.gov.uk/things-to-do/history-and-heritage/london-metropolitan-archives

speakoutlondon.org.uk

Nearest Tube: Barbican

The London Metropolitan Archives is the largest local authority record office in the UK, with 105 km of archives including audio recordings, printed materials and more. This includes a large selection of materials pertaining to LGBTQ+ history, lives and queer London. In 2014, they launched their 'Speak Out London – Diversity City' project, a community-led LGBTQ+ oral history initiative that has since mutated into the 'Speak Out London – Diversity City Archive'.

RUKUS! BLACK, LESBIAN, GAY, BISEXUAL AND TRANS (BLGBT) CULTURAL ARCHIVE

London Metropolitan Archives, 40 Northampton Rd, Farringdon, EC1R 0HB

cityoflondon.gov.uk/things-to-do/history-and-heritage/london-metropolitan-archives

Nearest Tube: Barbican

The rukus! Black, Lesbian, Gay, Bisexual and Trans (BLGBT) cultural archive was founded by photographer Ajamu X and filmmaker and theatre director Topher Campbell to chronicle and document the heritage, culture and experiences of Black LGBTQ+ people in the UK and around the world. Put together by rukus! Federation Limited; a programme of community-based work involving queer Black artists, activists and cultural producers; the archive is made up of diaries, letters, records, magazines, pamphlets, flyers, posters, journals, books, photographs and prints, audio-visual material, memorabilia and ephemera. It is accessible to the general public, though appointments must be made in advance.

QUEER TOURS OF LONDON – A MINCE THROUGH TIME

queertoursoflondon.com

Since 2017, Queer Tours of London have provided inquisitive queers and allies with a peek into London's LGBTQ+ past, shining a light on the often-overlooked lives and movements that make up the fabric of the city. Established by Dan Glass – activist, writer and historian – the organisation believes that understanding our queer past helps shape our queer future. Tours have explored the queer history of the West End, queer tours of Soho, LGBTQ+ migrant history, Section 28, the lesbian history of Brixton and walks around former gay district Earl's Court. Working with other organisations, such as Rebel Dykes and the African Rainbow Family, Queer Tours have campaigned for a permanent queer museum, hosted celebrations of cruising and the life of George Michael, and even organised a festival.

REBEL DYKES HISTORY PROJECT

rebeldykeshistoryproject.com

The Rebel Dykes History Project is an archive, art and film project that focuses on a group of young lesbians, the Rebel Dykes, who lived in London in the 1980s. A sexually liberated group, they were involved in various political movements throughout that period. Along with building an archive containing records, ephemera, art and printed materials, which will be housed at the Bishopsgate Institute, the Rebel Dykes History Project is also working on a documentary film. Headed up by activist, filmmaker and artist Siobhan Fahey, this group produces exhibitions, workshops, seminars and performances.

The Bishopsgate Institute, with its vast LGBTQ+ archive, is a stronghold of queer culture.

PRIDES

HACKNEY PRIDE 365
hackney.gov.uk/pride-365

Launched in 2017 by the local council, Hackney Pride 365 celebrates the area's diverse LGBTQ+ population with a number of community-led events. These include anything from club nights and queer walking tours to the annual Pride in the Park picnic at Stonebridge Gardens. Along with their own events programming, they have joined Pride in London and UK Black Pride, and have supported the annual Faggamuffin Bloc Party, a soundsystem run by queer people of colour.

PRIDE IN LONDON
prideinlondon.org

Pride in London is London's annual LGBTQ+ Pride event. Drawing around 1 million people each year, this festival centres on a huge, diverse parade that takes place on the Saturday of Pride weekend. The parade marches through central London, down Oxford Street and finishes at Trafalgar Square, where there is a stage for performances, speeches and more. In Soho they close the streets to traffic for a street party that sees each LGBTQ+ venue open its doors and blast music. There are several stages dotted around, including the Women's Stage, featuring more performances and speakers. This four-week festival includes exhibitions, picnics, sporting events, theatre

Trans Pride 2020.

productions, club nights, workshops and the annual Pride's Got Talent, which spotlights up-and-coming LGBTQ+ artists and performers.

UK BLACK PRIDE
ukblackpride.org.uk

For over 15 years, UK Black Pride has carved out a space for Black LGBTQ+ people and QTIPOC (queer, trans, intersex, people of colour). Co-founded by the venerable Lady Phyll, who now acts as executive director, it began life as a day trip to Southend-on-Sea for Black lesbians and bisexual women: an excursion so popular that one minibus' worth of people turned into three coach loads. Today, it is Europe's largest celebration for LGBTQ+ people of African, Asian, Caribbean, Middle Eastern and Latin American heritage. Held every summer during Pride – usually the Sunday after Pride in London – it is the highlight of the year for many LGBTQ+ people, a celebration of a multitude of intersecting communities, identities and backgrounds.

The official Pride festival event now takes place in Hackney. It's packed with speeches, performances, stalls from charities, food vendors and dancing. According to the charity Stonewall, over half of Black, Asian and minority ethnic LGBTQ+ people have experienced discrimination from within the LGBTQ+ community itself. Such sobering figures make the need for UK Black Pride, a safe space for Black LGBTQ+ people and QTIPOC, even more essential. As a result, the organisation's work isn't limited to Pride weekend: alongside the annual Pride festival, they also engage in social networking, community outreach and advocacy work, raising awareness for the experiences of the Black LGBTQ+ community. While Pride in London is often accused of being too corporate and centred on white, cisgender gay men, UK Black Pride is the opposite. It's a community-led reminder of the struggles that LGBTQ+ people still face, which uplifts and spotlights the different experiences of queer people from Black, Asian and other minority ethnic backgrounds.

WINTER PRIDE
winterprideuk.com

Every year at the Scala in King's Cross, Winter Pride serves up an indoor celebration of all things LGBTQ+, with an evening that brings together some of the best queer club nights and collectives under one roof. This ticketed event is more of a big queer knees-up than a political statement (although there remains something inherently political about thousands of LGBTQ+ people gathering to party). Previous years have seen the likes of cult queer club nights Mariah & Friendz, Gay Garage and R&She make appearances. Expect fancy dress, make-over stations, performances from drag artists, popstars and more.

ANDREW LUMSDEN

Andrew Lumsden has spent his life advocating and fighting for the rights of LGBTQ+ people. Born in Sutton in 1941, he is involved in LGBTQ+ activism to this day. Andrew became involved with the cause while working as a journalist at *The Daily Telegraph*. During this period, homosexuality was against the law, although the Sexual Offenses Act of 1967 partially changed this. Andrew was conscious of his sexuality by the age of 25, although he didn't come out widely until 1971. The year prior, he had read a news story about the Gay Liberation Front in *The Times*, where he was then working. He immediately sought out the organisation, who were at that time meeting on Wednesdays at the London School of Economics. Exhilarated by the encounter, he wrote an article in 1971 about the significance of this organisation. However, the editor of *The Times*, William Rees-Mogg, killed the feature. Unperturbed, Andrew took the article to *The Spectator*, who published it despite being a right-leaning magazine. Later that year, at a GLF meeting, he proposed that queer people needed their own newspaper – and thus the seeds for *Gay News* were sown.

The newspaper launched at Pride in 1972. Andrew wasn't a member of the group, led by Denis Lemon, who ran the publication. Instead, after years of journalistic work, he had immersed himself in queer activism, living in a drag commune in Bethnal Green. After getting arrested while protesting in Notting Hill, he spent some time in Los Angeles. He was living there when Harvey Milk, the first openly gay elected official in California, was assassinated in 1978. By the 1980s, Andrew had returned to the UK. When Denis Lemon announced his retirement from *Gay News*, Andrew stepped in. He edited the paper until it folded in 1983. The publication (with a readership of 20,000 LGBTQ+ folk) was one of the few LGBTQ+ workplaces where employees were split equally between men and women. Andrew later went to work at the *New Statesman*, although he was laid off in the '90s, along with the only other queer member of staff – a fact the National Union of Journalists ignored, when they complained. Infuriated by their dismissal, Andrew decided to emigrate to Spain and live off of his redundancy package. Andrew did eventually return to the UK. Over the past few years, he has spent his time giving talks about gay liberation and queer history. He met his partner, Stephen Clissold, at a gay reading group in 2006. Still a strong voice in LGBTQ+ activism, Andrew helped organise the 2020 celebrations for the 50th anniversary of the GLF in London.

HISTORY OF LONDON PRIDE

The first official Gay Pride Rally took place in London in 1972, two years after the first march in New York. Organised on the Saturday closest to the anniversary of the Stonewall Riots (which occurred in New York, 1969), around 2000 people attended the march, which headed down Oxford Street to Hyde Park. Prior to the 1972 rally, the Gay Liberation Front (GLF) had organised a number of demonstrations, the first being in 1970 at Highbury Fields. Gay Pride wasn't always appreciated by the city's queer community. Due to anti-LGBTQ+ attitudes, police persecution and the risk to personal safety, some people rejected the notion of a march outright. One year, when the march took place in Earl's Court, patrons of the infamous gay pub the Coleherne Arms threw beer cans at protesters. In 1981, following continuous police raids at the Gemini Club in Huddersfield, the Pride march was taken to West Yorkshire to support the local LGBTQ+ community in the north. The march was met by the far-right, fascist National Front. Ironically, the very police who had been hassling the local LGBTQ+ community then had to protect the protesters.

By the mid-'80s turnout to Pride had diminished; the 1984 march drew such small crowds the validity of the event came under question. A big organisational push saw next year's march burgeon, becoming the biggest at that point in the event's history with 10,000 attendees. The march, which set off from Hyde Park and ended up at Jubilee Gardens, was led by Lesbians and Gays Support the Miners. They were accompanied by several miners and their families, who they had raised money for during the miners' strike. In 1988, attendance rose again, with an estimated 40,000 people protesting the introduction of Section 28.

In the subsequent decade, London Pride (which was renamed Lesbian and Gay Pride in 1983 and then Lesbian, Gay, Bisexual and Transgender Pride in 1996) moved around the city, with day festivals that jumped from Brockwell Park to Clapham Common and Victoria Park. Pride underwent another change in 1999 when the event was rebranded London Mardi Gras, mimicking the Pride event that takes place in Sydney. While there was still a march, the main event was a festival in Finsbury Park. There was some controversy during this time that the festival, later named Big Gay Out, was a ticketed event, and by 2006 the festival ended.

Since then, London Pride has been the subject of scrutiny. In 2012, the city hosted World Pride – however, the start time for the march was moved last-minute, with LGBTQ+ activist Peter Tatchell suggesting this was a deliberate sabotage by the London Mayor's Office (then run by Boris Johnson). That same year, it became apparent that organisers had encountered financial difficulties, scaling down the festivities. The police informed venues in Soho that no extended licenses would be given out, and public consumption of alcohol was not allowed. As a result, the usually congested streets of Soho were eerily calm: no crowds of lively queers or sound systems blasting out bangers.

In 2013, a new governing body made up of people within the LGBTQ+ community, London LGBT+ Community Pride, successfully bid for the contract to organise Pride in London. By this point, attitudes to Pride had once again shifted, with accusations that its origins as a political protest had been smothered by corporations and partying. In recent years, complaints have arisen about the costs incurred to take part in the parade. Many

LGBTQ+ organisations and groups are unable to march – unlike brands like Tesco and Disney. The event has also been criticised for its lack of focus on the trans and bisexual communities, as well as not being a welcome space for queer people of colour.

This all came to a head in 2018 when a transphobic group were able to disrupt the parade. They led the march uninterrupted, handing out transphobic materials to the crowds. An open letter entitled 'Feminist solidarity: cis and trans people will not be divided' was published by LGBTQ+ leaders and activists to support the trans community. 'Pride itself has become a place for companies and organisations that have not historically played any part in the struggle for LGBTQIA+ rights, but now use the parade as a platform to sanitise their activities,' it read. 'Banks with deeply racist, colonial histories. Companies like G4S that run inhumane detention centres where many black and brown lesbian women are processed like cattle and sent back to the places they've experienced poverty and violence – the legacies of colonialism.'

That year, the UK's largest LGBTQ+ charity, Stonewall, also announced that they would no longer be taking part in Pride in London due to concerns over the event's 'lack of diversity'. 'We know this is an event that's important to many in our communities and very much hope to attend in future years,' they said in a statement. 'However last year [2018], Pride in London's community advisory board again raised concerns about the lack of diversity and inclusion at Pride in London – particularly of black and minority ethnic communities. Pride in London rejected these concerns from the community in the strongest terms and, as yet, have failed to make any public acknowledgement that they may need to make significant changes if Pride in London is to be an event for everyone.' Stonewall, instead, put their full support behind UK Black Pride.

Despite controversies, in 2019 Pride in London was attended by around 1.5 million people, making it the biggest Pride in the UK. Pride in London 2020 was cancelled due to the global coronavirus pandemic, set to return in 2021.

LADY PHYLL

When Phyll Opoku-Gyimah was growing up, she used to watch her grandmother working to support her local community. As a queer Black woman of Ghanaian descent, Phyll – known as Lady Phyll – came to understand the importance of safe spaces for individuals who live within the intersection of multiple oppressed identities. Her own intersecting identities have provided her with the lived experiences and knowledge to advocate and campaign for a better future.

Born in Islington, she has spent her life tackling discrimination and inequality. She began her career as a civil servant, before going to work for a trade union. It was here that she became the first Black senior lead negotiator, later taking on the role of head of political campaigns and equality. During this period, she co-founded Black Lesbians in the UK. What spaces there were for lesbians in London were overwhelmingly white, and Black lesbians and queer women needed somewhere to call their own. In 2004, the group, which so far had existed mainly in digital spaces, organised a trip to Southend-on-Sea. It proved so popular that the minibus-sized group grew into three-coach loads of Black queer women. Lady Phyll realised there was a need for spaces and events that centred and celebrated queer Black people and QTIPOC, so in 2005, she organised the first UK Black Pride. The event drew around 200 people – but since then, UK Black Pride has only grown. In 2019, the crowds numbered 10,000. Black Pride has become an integral and essential event for London's LGBTQ+ community, especially Black LGBTQ+ people and QTIPOC.

In 2016, Phyll was nominated for an MBE, which she refused, citing the UK's homophobic, colonial legacy. 'I don't believe in empire. I don't believe in, and actively resist, colonialism and its toxic and enduring legacy in the Commonwealth, where – among many other injustices – LGBTQI people are still being persecuted, tortured and even killed because of sodomy laws, including in Ghana, where I am from, that were put in place by British imperialists,' she said at the time. Her decision to turn down the MBE, however, resulted in the moniker that she goes by today: Lady Phyll. She made history once more in 2019 when she was appointed as the executive director of the Kaleidoscope Trust, becoming the first Black woman in the UK to lead an LGBTQ+ human rights organisation. She acts as a patron of akt, an LGBT+ homeless charity, as well as being the director of UK Black Pride and a columnist for Diva magazine – and a mother to her daughter. Lady Phyll dreams of moving to the Caribbean, where she can put her feet up. Let's be honest: she deserves it.

ISBN: 9781788841023

British Library Cataloguing-in-Publication Data
A catalogue record for this book is available from the British
Library

The author and publisher gratefully acknowledge the permission
granted to reproduce the copyright material in this book. Every
effort has been made to trace copyright holders and to obtain
their permission for the use of copyright material. The publisher
apologises for any errors or omissions in the text and would be
grateful if notified of any corrections that should be incorporated
in future reprints or editions of this book.

Design concept: Webb & Webb Design Ltd.

Front cover: The roofline of the Two Brewers, Clapham High Street.
Back cover: Legendary troupe, Sink the Pink, in the doorway of
The Glory, Kingsland Road.
Frontispiece: Old Compton Street, in the heart of Soho.
Pages 4-5: A zebra crossing reimagined for Pride.

MIX
Paper from
responsible sources
FSC® C124385
www.fsc.org

Printed in China
for ACC Art Books Ltd., Woodbridge, Suffolk, England

www.accartbooks.com

Acknowledgements
Queer London would be nothing without LGBTQ+ historians and
writers Matt Cook, Matt Houlbrook, Alakarim Jivani, Peter Burton,
Stuart Feather, Tony Walton, Jill Gardiner and Peter Ackroyd,
whose work has proved essential to the formation of this book.
Thank you to Catriona McAvoy, Amanda Freeman, Lisa Power,
Kat Hudson, Dan Beaumont, Paul Flynn, Lavinia Co-op, Princess
Julia, Patrick Black, Lyall Hakaraia, Luke Howard, Siobhan Fahey,
Justin Bengry, Peter Robinson, Sue Sanders, Sarah Moore, Rhys
Thomas, Josh Rivers, Anna Harvey, Glyn Fussell, Stacey Dale,
Michael Smith, Tom Mehrtens, K Bailey Obazee, John Sizzle
and the staff at the Bishopsgate Institute. Thank you to all the
incredible LGBTQ+ people who feature in this book – you are my
inspiration, and I am so honoured that you sat for portraits and
answered my questions. Without Tim Boddy, this book would
not be as beautiful as it is, and I will always be grateful for your
enthusiasm, flexibility and talent. Thank you to Andrew Whittaker
at ACC Art books, who perhaps didn't know what he was getting
himself into when he approached me to write *Queer London*, but
who has been patient and kind during unprecedented times. Also
to Craig Holden, and the wonderful Bryn Porter, who has shaped
this book into what it is today, thank you. Finally, my thanks to
David, Kate, Douglas, Sophia, Grace, Tom, Lukas, Lauren, Jess
and my family.

**ACC
ART
BOOKS**